POETRY CO

GW00720725

GREAT MINDS

From North & East Yorkshire
Edited by Steve Twelvetree

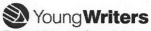 Young**Writers**

First published in Great Britain in 2005 by:
Young Writers
Remus House
Coltsfoot Drive
Peterborough
PE2 9JX
Telephone: 01733 890066
Website: www.youngwriters.co.uk

SB ISBN 1 84460 705 4

Foreword

This year, the Young Writers' 'Great Minds' competition proudly presents a showcase of the best poetic talent selected from over 40,000 up-and-coming writers nationwide.

Young Writers was established in 1991 to promote the reading and writing of poetry within schools and to the youth of today. Our books nurture and inspire confidence in the ability of young writers and provide a snapshot of poems written in schools and at home by budding poets of the future.

The thought, effort, imagination and hard work put into each poem impressed us all and the task of selecting poems was a difficult but nevertheless enjoyable experience.

We hope you are as pleased as we are with the final selection and that you and your family continue to be entertained with *Great Minds From North & East Yorkshire* for many years to come.

Contents

Breckenbrough School, Thirsk

Cottingham High School, Cottingham

Rachel Noble (13)	77
Kirsty Bennett (12)	78

Ripon Grammar School, Ripon

Emily Walden (11)	78
Rafa Alam (17)	79
Richard Delf (11)	80
James Simmons (11)	80
Rachael Sharp (11)	81
Georgina Burnett (11)	81
Gabriella Ireland (15)	82
Sally Jones (11)	82
Danielle Graham (12)	83
Paul Midgley (16)	84
Adam Robinson (11)	84
Natalie Turner (11)	85
Giles Pitts (12)	86
Ella Stelling (11)	87
Alex Warriner (11)	88
Robin Whitfield (11)	88
Maddy Olley (12)	89
Isobel Mitchell (11)	89
Katie Wade (11)	90
Jack Richards (12)	90
Jodie Simpson (12)	91
Louiza Whiteley (11)	91
Jonathan Walker (12)	92
Guy Buckle (11)	92
Yasmin Rogers (12)	93
Christian Hair (11)	93
Eloise Robinson (12)	94
Rachel Osborne (11)	95
Freya Mortimer (11)	96
Jonathan Coates (11)	96
Jessica Priestley (13)	97
Rachel Cunningham (14)	97
Nicole Hutton (13)	98
Kiera Chapman (12)	98
Jessica Burgess (11)	99
Rosie Tattersall (12)	99
Clare Burnett (13)	100

Alec Graham (11)	100
Jack Park (12)	101
Natalia de Hutiray (12)	101
Hannah Olsen Shaw (11)	102
Adam Lister (15)	102
Leanne Hanrahan (15)	103
Frances Shaw (12)	103
Lauren Fielding (15)	104
Emily Davies (14)	105
Jess Warren (14)	106
Dave Marsden (14)	106
Charlotte Frank (12)	107
Carrie Turner-Fryatt (12)	107
Alison Fraser (15)	108
James Clarke (13)	109
Maggie Ellis (15)	110
Emily Cottrell (15)	111
Amber Gilliam (15)	112
Luke Haggerty (12)	113
Jamie Horn (15)	114
Sophie McEvoy (14)	115
Katie Fortune (14)	116
Joseph Priestley (12)	116
Edward Lilley (14)	117
Ben Wright (13)	117
Theo Parker (11)	118
Megan Wright (13)	119
Liam Evans (11)	120
Charlie Stelling (12)	120
Isobel Jennings (11)	121
Edward Riley (12)	122
Greg Munsch (12)	123
Thomas King (11)	124
Jessica Lyall (11)	125
Polly Sands (13)	126
Helen Anderson (11)	127
Amelia Tearle (12)	128
Joe Turner (12)	129
Joshua Hill (12)	129
Alicia Hunt (11)	130
Brooke Farrar (14)	130
Rory Buckle (11)	131

Ryedale School, York

Bryony Gillespie (12)	181
Amy Collier (11)	182
Charlotte Fairweather (11)	182
Ruby Williams (11)	183
Alistair Holmes (11)	183
Robert Thurlow (11)	184
Suzanne Jefferson (11)	184
Charlotte Collier (11)	185
Louise Smith (11)	185
Philippa Adderley (11)	186
Christie Hewitt (11)	186
Rufus Brooks (12)	186
Jonny Pattenden (11)	187
Phoebe Maxwell (11)	187
Jimmy Goode (11)	188
Antonia Clark (11)	188
Rosie Hayman (11)	189
Heather Weston (11)	189
Elisa Caton (11)	190
Meg Holmes (11)	190
Emma Bumby (11)	191
Gail Humpleby (11)	191
Harry Wright (11)	192
Megan Brown (11)	193

St Mary's Catholic High School, Grimsby

Bryony Watson (11)	193
Nichola Robinson (13)	194
Mollie Robertson (11)	194
Leanne Fothergill (12)	195
Charlotte Rogers (11)	195
Tom Pell (12)	196

The Forest School, Knaresborough

Chris Goodier (14)	196
Kyle Watson (12)	196
Michael Riley	197
Isobel Chapman (13)	197
Jessica Gregory	197

The Poems

School

My first day at school was scary
Because of this girl called Mary
She pushed me around
And hangs in a big crowd
Her hair's a mess like a bushy bee
I wish it was full of buzzy bees
They wanted a pen fight
Because they said I was too bright
They told me to get a bath
And embarrassed me in maths
The classrooms are dull
And the teachers are like bulls
School's like a hutch
Locked in is too much
They put my work in the bin
Oh, what a state I'm in
I don't think I'm a fool
Cos I always go to school
They said I'm a Billy
But I've got a friend called Milly.

Sophie Guymer
Archbishop Thurstan CE (VC) School, Bilton Grange

Hull Fair

H ull fair is fantastic,
U p and down the rides go fast,
L ike a person yelling on the rides,
L ike them chuckling when the rides go up and down.

F air has thousands of rides,
A ll the people yelling and shouting,
I love Hull fair,
R ides are speedy and fun.

Rebecca Machray
Archbishop Thurstan CE (VC) School, Bilton Grange

Clouds

As white as snow
As light as air
These that wander by
Like tiny little islands
Floating in the sky

Look up there
In the sky so blue
As fluffy as a bear
It's staring down on you

A dragon hiding in its lair
A horse's tail
A lion's hair
Claws razor-sharp like a bear

As white as snow
As light as air
These that wander by
Like tiny little islands
Floating in the sky.

Sammy-Jo Gilbey (13)
Archbishop Thurstan CE (VC) School, Bilton Grange

Hull Fair

H ull fair is so big, like the moon,
U nder the ride they are moving things,
L ollipops are so yummy,
L ights at Hull fair are so groovy.

F air is so greatly enormous,
A ll the rides at Hull fair are extraordinary and fabulous,
I think Hull fair is fantastic but they take all your money,
R ides at Hull fair, I'm such an admirer.

Rachel Amanda Bird (11)
Archbishop Thurstan CE (VC) School, Bilton Grange

The Baby Of My Family

I can't forget the day Tyler was born
His tiny feet
Looked good enough to eat
I can remember the day Tyler was born

I can't forget the day Tyler was born
His moses cot
He slept a lot
I can remember the day Tyler was born

I can't forget the day Tyler was born
He looked so cute
His sound was mute
I can remember the day Tyler was born

I can't forget the day Tyler was born
He slept in peace
He had no teeth
I can remember the day Tyler was born.

Karl Stevens (12)
Archbishop Thurstan CE (VC) School, Bilton Grange

Hull Fair

H ull fair is the best fair ever
U known rides which are new
L ights that you see
L ift-off in the Big Ben

F un as you arrive in the funhouse
A live, the fair is alive
I love the funhouse
R ides that go up and down.

Ricky Thompson
Archbishop Thurstan CE (VC) School, Bilton Grange

My Little Sister

Here's my sister all small in her cot
Her name is Holly-May and she sleeps a lot
And I love her a lot

She just lies there having the easy life
She opens her eyes and looks at me
But then she cries and then poops!

Everyone is happy, then she lies in her cot
But now five years on
She screams and nips
Bites and pulls hair but that's not new

Here is something a baby does:
Eat
Sleep
And poop

But now five years on
I still love her
Though she's a devil!

Danielle Spencer (11)
Archbishop Thurstan CE (VC) School, Bilton Grange

Hull Fair

H ull fair is the best place
U nder all the rides the bell will ring
L aughing on the rides
L ights are like being in Heaven

F un rides are the best
A ll the people shout
I n the toilets it's stinky
R ides are simply the best things in the world
    because they go upside down, I went on the Eclipse.

Ashley Hakeney (11)
Archbishop Thurstan CE (VC) School, Bilton Grange

When I Went To Torquay

When I went on holiday,
I went to the zoo and saw a wallaby,
I also saw a monkey,
Which was really funky,
Then I saw my mate,
It was quite late.

Then I went in the pool,
Which was really cool,
I went splish and splash,
It looked like a crash,
Then I went on the boat,
So that I would float.

Then I went on the sand,
Which was a big land,
Then I went on some rides
And some really big slides.

The sun was shining bright,
It was very light,
Then we had to go home,
So I started to moan.

Demi Wright
Archbishop Thurstan CE (VC) School, Bilton Grange

Hull Fair

H ull fair is boring
U pside down rides are fast
L ots of lovely food
L iquorice whips are disgusting

F air only comes once a year
A lot of rubbish on the roads
I love winning prizes on the stalls
R ides are scary!

Elliott Taylor (11)
Archbishop Thurstan CE (VC) School, Bilton Grange

My Holiday

I'm going on holiday
And on a boat,
I can't wait to get away,
We're riding on a moat.

I can see the Eiffel Tower,
Oh my goodness, it's big,
There's a Disney character
And he's wearing a wig.

Gosh, it's really hot here
And the sun is bright,
I'm gonna have a beer,
To keep me through the night.

Now we're on the fifth day
And now I'm going home,
The coach driver's name is Jay,
Oh and my mum has bought a gnome.

Karla Liegh Burrill (11)
Archbishop Thurstan CE (VC) School, Bilton Grange

Hull Fair

H ull fair is boring and it is too much money
   but you can buy candyfloss
U nhappy Hull fair was because they were leaving Hull
L oud music and blaring lights
L ovely coloured stalls shining so bright

F antastic food that smells so great
A nd lots of candyfloss that I ate
I hate the fair like I hate my brother, Jordan
R apid rides like the wind, I am scared that I might fall off.

Shaunna Dixon
Archbishop Thurstan CE (VC) School, Bilton Grange

My Little Sis!

It was my sister's first day at home,
I bet she felt a bit alone,
Because she only knew my mum,
Now all she does is play with her thumb.

Now that she's two,
She goes for a wee on the loo
'Cause she thinks that she's a big girl,
She looks so cute with that great curl.

She is very, very naughty,
Also really, really sporty,
She always cries for me
And she loves her cups of tea.

She is a little devil,
She loves drinking brevel,
She loves playing with her toys,
Also she chases lots of boys.

Jade Travis
Archbishop Thurstan CE (VC) School, Bilton Grange

Hull Fair

H ull fair is a very happy place,
U pside down rides go like a spinning wheel,
L ick a beautiful lolly as big as the sun,
L ovely smells drift towards me like the wind.

F un rides that make you sick,
A fter rides I have a drink,
I go on another ride,
R ides at Hull fair are very fun like a day out.

Lauren Skelton
Archbishop Thurstan CE (VC) School, Bilton Grange

Buffy

A bundle of mischief on the run,
Hiding and looking for fun,
She's chasing birds and climbing trees,
Hunting mice for something to tease.

Her fur is so soft when I stroke her,
She purrs and she runs all around,
She leaps up the stairs,
Her little ears twitch when we call her.

She wrinkles her nose when we fetch out her bed,
She doesn't like dogs,
She scratches and hisses,
She wriggles when you tickle her.

She's cute,
We love Buffy the cat,
Especially in the night-time
When she's asleep having her nap.

Hannah Hill
Archbishop Thurstan CE (VC) School, Bilton Grange

Hull Fair

H ull fair is as big as the sun,
U p and down the ride just like the sun,
L oud and quiet the music goes just like the people talking,
L iquorice, liquorice, you can taste the flavours and smells really fruity

F air rides go round and round just like a roundabout,
A pples and toffee apples, you can taste it and it's just like glue,
I see the lights shining bright when the sun comes out,
R oller coasters go round and round, just like a really
                                        fast roundabout.

Vicki Pratt (11)
Archbishop Thurstan CE (VC) School, Bilton Grange

The Dwarf On Fire

I'm all excited,
My sister's delighted,
I hope it's fun,
Hurry up, Mum!

We went through the hallway,
Up the stairs, all the way,
The flames were dazzling,
The old fogies were hassling.

The dwarf came, he was on fire,
Believe me, it was on his own desire.
He jumped in the water,
He looked like an otter.

After that we had a meal,
The man on fire looked like an eel.
We ate with our bare hands,
It was fresh from the pans.

Jack Ingleson (11)
Archbishop Thurstan CE (VC) School, Bilton Grange

Hull Fair

H ull fair is so good, I can feel the wind on my hand,
U p and down, the rides bring joy to my heart,
L ots of people going on rides, I can't hear my voice speaking,
L ate nights are very late but not like night.

F ear is in little kids' faces when they enter the haunted
house and I'm scared too,
A ride is like a race, going fast,
I nto the funhouse I go, when I come out I'm so dizzy,
R iders come and go when I go on them.

Nathan Ritchie (11)
Archbishop Thurstan CE (VC) School, Bilton Grange

Babies, Babies . . .

There she was crying in her crib,
Wriggling around,
Playing with her bib.

She punched through the air,
Crying tears of joy,
I took her out and sat her near the bear.

She wriggled and giggled,
Chewed on a biscuit,
She started to nibble it.

She cried and cried,
Until it was time to go home,
I went to bed feeling happy, not glum.

Amanda Lyon (12)
Archbishop Thurstan CE (VC) School, Bilton Grange

Hull Fair!

Excited and happy butterflies in my tummy
I went with my daddy and mummy
It was very, very loud
In the sky, not a cloud

Candyfloss, snap, crackle and pop
The ride I went on went right to the top
There was loads of lights
And tons of frights

I met my mates
They were very late
We went on a ride
Then we decided to hide.

Charlotte Barrett
Archbishop Thurstan CE (VC) School, Bilton Grange

Primary Colours

She dropped me off, my mum that is,
I felt my tummy bubble and fizz.
The start of school, today's the day,
I felt the urge to run away!

The teacher emerged from the school front door,
Greeting children four by four.
Mrs West she's called, a very nice lady,
She held my hand, I nearly went crazy!

We entered the classroom hand in hand,
I saw spillages of water and heads full of sand.
I was about to turn and run away,
When a group of children asked me to play.

We played with the puzzles and read all the books,
While a group of boys gave us all funny looks.
My new friends' names were Savannah and Lottie,
I could tell by their faces, the boys would be snotty!

At playtime the playground was full of dead leaves,
All beautifully drifting, among the September breeze.
The children were playing all different games,
The boys playing football and girls chasing James!

At dinner, we ate all of our packed lunch,
We went in the playground and crackled and crunched.
First we threw leaf bombs, then we played tig,
Then I went and tripped over a twig!

The afternoon came, it was time to go home,
I wanted to stay, I started to groan.
My dad picked me up, along with my mum,
I just couldn't wait for tomorrow to come!

Samantha Laverack (11)
Archbishop Thurstan CE (VC) School, Bilton Grange

School

School is as evil as the Devil himself
The school traps you in the endless maze
Filled with endless upon endless of deadly traps
You try and find your way out of the magical illusions
Holding you trapped in this devil of a dungeon

The Devil sends his army of death
To execute you and eat you limb from limb
Sucking you dry of your blood
Ripping into your heart and eating it
Like they had never been fed
The evil birds eat your leftovers then leave

The teachers come and suck up your souls
Feeding on the dead
The cooks in the canteen cooking your liver
And your heart.

Joshua Norman
Archbishop Thurstan CE (VC) School, Bilton Grange

Untitled

I ran into the house, didn't care
Gunfire came as a vision glare
Sat down, didn't know what to do
Had to abandon my Mafia crew
Triad's members shot me in the face
Battered me all over the place
All they cared about was watching me die
The four horsemen drawing nigh
I fell down with the sound of smashing glass
They had took my pain threshold to the mass
I can see my vision fading fast
Now I know this day was my last.

Dane Crosby (13)
Archbishop Thurstan CE (VC) School, Bilton Grange

My Dog, Holly

She laid there looking shy
Oh how the world does pass her by!
Laying there on the mat
I wish I had a life like that

Her nickname was Holly and the loo
Because every five minutes she needed a poo!
Every day she always got toys
Even though she barks at boys

She snores away
Almost every day
She bites her rugs
And tugs and tugs

Her birthday's in October
Even though she never gets sober!
She can really run
Although she weighs a ton.

Connor Kearns (11)
Archbishop Thurstan CE (VC) School, Bilton Grange

Please Help Me!

Bullies, I hate them,
They're really bad
And make me sad.
I cry and cry when I get hit,
But it's only a bit,
They pick on me
And call me names,
Then spoil my games,
So I moan and groan,
Until I see them *again!*

June Agnew (13)
Archbishop Thurstan CE (VC) School, Bilton Grange

My Best Friend

My teacher told us to write an essay,
On which I must detest.
She told us to write about,
Which friend I like the best.

We had to write about one person,
One person and that's it.
I didn't want to do that,
So I sat there, I sit.

Then my teacher comes up to me,
Looking angry she says,
'Dear, come on work,
Or I'll make you write more essays!'

So I start to think about,
Which friend I like the best.
But when I finally pick one,
I think about the rest.

So I finally start writing,
On which friend I like the best.
But then Miss shouts,
'It's home time, take a rest.'

No, I won't take a rest,
I want to make it good.
I want to make it really great,
Because it's about my bestest bud.

So I hand it into my teacher, she says,
'Dear, you've done it all wrong.'
I reply, 'I've got more than one best friend,
I've got a list very, very long.'

Laura Scaife (12)
Archbishop Thurstan CE (VC) School, Bilton Grange

When Mason Was Born

I can remember when Mason was born
He was as heavy as a bag of corn
When I saw him in his cot
He seemed to sleep a lot

I will never forget when Mason was born
Those eyes were so cute
When he was born
He was in his birthday suit

When Mason was born
In the early morn
The sunset was just rising
And the news was surprising.

Jonathan Baron
Archbishop Thurstan CE (VC) School, Bilton Grange

Sun To The Moon

It's the day
So it's time to play
Games and fun
In the sun

Sun to the moon
It will all be gone soon
It's dark and cold at night
There is no more light

It's time for bed
So rest your sleepy head
You don't want to yawn
At the new dawn.

Rachel Oliphant (11)
Barlby High School, Selby

The Anger Deep Inside

The anger deep inside she felt,
Like newborn flames it would not melt.
It was always there, it would never go.
She tried so hard not to let it show.

Her world became a darkened well,
But no one, she would ever tell,
Of the pain she felt inside,
It became too much to abide.

One day her life began to fall,
She was an outcast, no friends at all.
She began to wish herself away,
You could see the change day by day.

A part of her would change and die,
She disappeared with no goodbye.
She was a person who knew no better,
If only I had never met her.

Lucie Stanworth (12)
Barlby High School, Selby

My Life

S un and then rain beats down on my head,
T urned my green coat to a nice shiny red,
R eady to be picked and to meet my fate,
A ll I could do was to wonder and wait,
W here would I go? What would I be?
B et it's to a party or for royalty's tea,
E veryone wants me, it's just like a dream,
R ich people love me with champagne and cream,
R ed was my colour and now I am pink,
Y ou wanted a milkshake and now I'm your drink.

Nykysha Young (11)
Barlby High School, Selby

Blowing In The Wind

Blowing in the wind
With his ashes scattered
Soon he'll be hard to find

He didn't like to be this way
He shut his eyes and dreamed

Back to when he was dying on a hospital bed
Connected with a life-support machine

He didn't like to be this way
He shut his eyes and dreamed

Back to when he was in the old people's home
Where you had to stay in bed all day

He didn't like it this way
He shut his eyes and dreamed

Back to when he was young and happy
And nothing went wrong

He liked to be this way
He dreamed hard to try and stay there.

Richie Salter (11)
Barlby High School, Selby

Hunger

Hunger is the colour of green like a vegetable
It tastes like a potato with rotten peel
It feels like achy pain
It smells like a chocolate delight

It looks like a miserable person that can't move
It reminds you of your mum torturing you
It sounds like the rumble of an earthquake.

Stuart Swan (11)
Barlby High School, Selby

Chocolate Bar Crumb Dreaming

Chocolate bar crumbs, laying in the dark, dusty vacuum,
She was a full bar, but now a bit.
Soon there would be visitors which were creepy-crawlies.

She didn't like the way she was now,
She longed to be the way she was before.

Back to when she was full,
But starting to melt,
A mouth ready to take a juicy bite.

She didn't like the way she was now,
She longed to be the way she was before.

Next to her friends, she longed to stay,
Happy in her shining wrapper,
Being picked, she started to cry.

She didn't like the way she was now,
She longed to be the way she was before.

Happy in the factory,
Fresh and new she was,
Then came the hot oven which only filled
Her with bad thoughts.

She didn't like the way she was now,
She longed to be the way she was before.

In the basket, only young,
Taken away from her family,
She was just a helpless seed.

She didn't like the way she was now,
She longed to be the way she was before.

Now she was happy,
Ready, fresh, born
Joyfully lying as a cocoa bean.

She loved the way she was before,
If only her past was now,
It's all she longed for.

Alicia Cox (12)
Barlby High School, Selby

Killer Animals

The slimy, scaly snake,
Slithering through the
Green, silky grass.

Waiting to get you.

The lazy, luxurious lion,
Leapt over the brown,
Soggy log.

Waiting to get you.

The clever, curious cat,
Claws at the clean carpet
With pride.

After he killed you!

Liam King (11)
Barlby High School, Selby

Fright

Fright lurks in the shadows,
It hides behind the door,
It's hiding in the cupboard,
It's beneath the floor.

You can never see it,
But you can be assured,
When you are least expecting it,
Fright is at your door.

Rhys Chamberlain (11)
Barlby High School, Selby

Happiness

Happiness is blue like the endless sky.
Happiness smells like the cool fresh air.
Happiness tastes like a red sweet strawberry.
Happiness sounds like the little robins singing high up in the tree.
Happiness looks like the countryside covered in flowers.
Happiness feels like someone has given you a million pounds
for your birthday.
Happiness reminds me of my first goal.

Mathew Taylor (11)
Barlby High School, Selby

Is . . .

Is there life in outer space
That looks just like the human race?
Is there any reason for war
Other than killing and explosions galore?
Is there always a time and place
For every soul and every place?
Is there reason for everything
For every good deed and every sin?
Is there really a meaning to life?
If so, why kill each other with a gun or knife?
Is life and reality always fair
Or are we meant to shout and blare?
Is it necessary for things to be known
And things kept secret and unknown?
Is it necessary for me at school to write this poem?
In fact, it isn't, so I'm stopping and going home.

James Suddes (13)
Breckenbrough School, Thirsk

War At Winter

A surgeon in the field was I
In the cold, hard thick of warfare
To aid the troops as for freedom they strived
As the foe did rip and tear

'Twas the final night we were at war
Soulless bodies lay all around
I still remember such horrific gore
Yet later, there was not a sound

The tanks, we heard them rolling forth
No man could bear the sound
As explosions sounded from the north
There was panic all around

Finally, at long awaited last
The debris was to clear
The men returned to their homeland so fast
To celebrate with food and beer

We hope we shall never return to war
Every man hopes to see it never
And that dreaded night of blood and gore
Is behind us now forever.

Darren Wood (13)
Breckenbrough School, Thirsk

The Everlasting Tree Of Hope

The everlasting tree of hope
Hangs over the world below
The killings, the theft and the hurt, are tragic
If only one could pluck a piece of fruit
From the everlasting tree of hope
What would the world be like today?

Tom Wynn (14)
Breckenbrough School, Thirsk

Pip

There was a lad called Pip
Who was giving me jip
So I bust his lip
Kicked him in his hip
Went to his knees
And he kept on saying
Please, please, please
So I kicked him to the floor
Stamped on his jaw
He was screaming
No more, no more
That would teach him for being hardcore!

Mark Leach (14)
Breckenbrough School, Thirsk

My Poem Memories

I lay awake excitedly
Waiting till I hear the lovely sound
Of seagulls squawking
In my head like an alarm clock ringing
Looking out of the window
Staring out at the glistening sea

Watching speedboats speeding past
Waves crashing, smashing
Against children's legs
I want to be out there
Can't . . . ill
Memories to treasure

Remembering the past
But now I'm in hospital
I've got food poisoning,
Dreaming of sun, sea and sand.

Abbie Rowland (12)
Cottingham High School, Cottingham

As I Die

As light slips into darkness
I'm lying here in your arms
As noise turns to silence
I'm drowning here in your charms
As my vision begins to blur
I feel your heart beat fast
As my blood begins to run cold
I reflect on our long past

As my lips turn slightly blue
I feel you hold me tight
As my skin goes really pale
I feel no need to fight
As my body begins to weaken
I'm taking my last breath
As I gaze into your eyes one last time
I know there's nothing of me left

As you kiss my cold white forehead
I long to be back there with you
As a tear falls down your cheek
I know you feel the same way too
As you lay me down to rest
I am already flying up high
As you feel cold all around you
I am saying my goodbye

As you hold a knife towards you
I beg but you don't hear
As you fall across the floor
I scream, I'm full of fear
As I kneel down by your side
Your body is reignited
As I feel your lips touch mine
We are reunited.

Chloe Nelson (15)
Cottingham High School, Cottingham

My Man U Shirt

I'm on my way to watch Man U,
Wearing my brand new shirt,
It's really soft and ace to wear,
Because it's the best one yet.

Red and white,
Glowing like the boiling sun in Turkey,
Thousands of us pouring in old Trafford,
Like water out of a tap.

But as I stand at the turnstile,
Thinking of young children, same age as me,
Working in a horrid factory in China.

From dawn to dusk,
Making shirts just for us.
I
  M
   A
    G
    I
     N
      E
       that
Not being able to go to school
Not having an education

My Man U shirt just won't be the same
Because of how it's made
All of those poor little kids
When I wear my Man U shirt
I will feel really bad.

Stacey Celik (12)
Cottingham High School, Cottingham

Love's Promise

Love notes exchanged in class,
Kisses given lying in the grass,
Holding hands in the park,
Walking home after dark,
Counting stars in the midnight sky,
Trying to get our kite to fly,
Your scent clinging to me,
Sharing a chair, perched on your knee,
Eating ice cream in mid-December,
Important dates you forget to remember,
Running through puddles in the pouring rain,
Snuggled up together, sat on a train,
Giggling on the back row of the pictures,
Shouting from the sidelines at all your fixtures,
Crying when you buy me flowers,
Always on the phone for hours,
Singing badly to 'our song',
Cheering when you admit you're wrong,
I remember every little thing
And that is why I wear this ring,
When I said I'd be your wife,
I promised I'd be here for life,
I love you with all my heart
And I promise that we'll never part,
I'll never ever let you go
And I hope that you will always know,
That come what may,
I'll love you 'til my dying day,
Because you take my breath away.

Alexandra Bristow
Cottingham High School, Cottingham

The Man

Fiery-red like the crimson of a serpent's tongue,
that's what anger is to me . . .

It flows through your veins
and drives you insane.

You look it in the eyes
and you can see nothing staring back.

It slaps you hard across the face,
the taste of dirty blood in your mouth.

It screeches and screams,
penetrating your eardrums.

You are knocked to the black, marble floor,
your head swirling ferociously.

Anger . . .

Andrew Gilroy (14)
Cottingham High School, Cottingham

Like A Lioness

Like a wild, un-mild, lone lioness
Like the fawn of Sagittarius
Like a manipulative masseuse
Like a poisonous, putrid juice

It will seep beneath your veins
Causing happiness and pain
As you try to sustain your brain
Though you know your efforts are in vain

Love can make you have to choose
But against love should you win or lose
When it can weigh you down like pneumonia
Yet be blissful pandemonium

It can wholly devour your positiveness
Love is like a lioness.

Catherine Kay (14)
Cottingham High School, Cottingham

A School Day

You trudge up the side
Of a mountain in the Alps
You put the skis on your feet
And skim back down the mountain

Suddenly you're on a beach
And a bird is singing
But now it looks more like a clock
And the sound it makes is beeping

The sand that you were standing on
Turns white and slaps you in the face
You open your eyes and you can feel
The pillows and sheets are calling, calling

They want you to rest and go to sleep
And enjoy oblivion, but you resist
You reach across and turn the alarm off
Your brain is asleep but you cannot

You pull on your clothes
And pack your bags, eat
Some toast and pull on
Your coat . . .

Another boring school day.

Peter Jonas (12)
Cottingham High School, Cottingham

Love

Love is red because it is deep.

It sounds like a couple laughing together.
It tastes like strawberries and cream.
It smells like a freshly picked bunch of flowers.

You can see love between couples in the street.

Love feels warm and makes you happy.
Love reminds me of a rose.

Kristina Amaira (14)
Cottingham High School, Cottingham

Stone Cold

India, ah another beautiful baking-hot
Morning in the city of Calcutta
I splash cold water over my face
Comb my hair and get dressed

I'm glad I'm away from the noise of Hull
Even if I am in another city
I think I'll tour it
Yes, I haven't done that yet

It's another restless day
For the tired taxi drivers
I walk down to the port, fishermen
Fishing as usual, fishing as still as can be
They're sculpted into a statue
With their rods out to sea

I look out upon the sea
There is an island out there
I think I'll take a look
Yes, I haven't done that yet

I arrive, there are lots of huts
I look in one, a man tries to stop me
He's holding a gun, but I get a glimpse
A boy, no older than seven
He's sewing balls and shirts
He's crying . . .

Ah, I'm back in Hull
I think I'll go see my children
Yes, I haven't done that yet.

Robert Gillingwater (12)
Cottingham High School, Cottingham

Holiday Girl

Morning time is here
And holiday girl has woken,
Hearing the sound of the waves,
Lapping up against the shore.

Wild birds crying as they fly,
Fish jumping out of the water,
Fishermen going out to sea
And children out to sea.

Women bustling and chatting,
Yap, yap, yapping as they work,
The sun has risen fully out of the sky,
Morning time is here.

Groggily, groggily.

Morning time is here,
Holiday girl has woken
Hearing the sound of people coming,
People going.

Pigeons roosting on the hospital roof,
The goldfish swimming in the bowl,
Businessmen zooming past in their cars
And children shouting as they go to school.

Nurses bustling and chatting,
Yap, yap, yapping as they work,
The sun has risen out of the sky,
Morning time is here,
Another hospital day.

Hannah Dodson (12)
Cottingham High School, Cottingham

Morning

Morning
And the bright little girl
Wakes up to the sound
Of people having fun
In her bright mind

The elderly
Creeping down the stairs
To breakfast
Trying not to make a noise
What a sad sound in the morning

Young children
Talking to their mums
Saying what they want
For their breakfast

She could hear shouting
From people surrounding her
'Get up! Get up!' cried her mother

To another school day!

Stephanie North (12)
Cottingham High School, Cottingham

Noise

I like noise . . .
The swish of a sound, the thud of a mace
The rush of cavalry on a race
The bang of a shield, the length of pikes
The army of steel as it hikes
The roar of lions, the call of the judge
The hit of a bear is more than a nudge
The boom of cannons, the bosh of guns
The gasp of air reaches the lungs
The twang of bows, the grain on a wheel
The roar of men on the battlefield
I like noise.

Edward Greenall (11)
Cottingham High School, Cottingham

Homework

Your attention please class,
Your homework for today
The 20 questions on page 101
This must be completed by Tuesday 26th
If not completed
Then there will be trouble
Detentions give out
Letters home
Talks with parents
Some people will complete
Some people won't complete
For them who complete
Prepare to be praised
For them who don't complete
Prepare to be punished
Make sure you put it in your diary
If you have trouble
Please see me
I'll be in M2 every day
There goes the bell
Class dismissed.

Liam Partis (13)
Cottingham High School, Cottingham

Noise

The flap of a bird, the snap of a stick,
The whoosh of a train on a rusty old rail,
The flush of a chain, the rack of my brain,
The boom of a bomb, the snort of a pig,
The drip of the tap, the crash of a car,
The bash of a wave, the crack of a gun,
The shut of a door, as it slams and bangs,
The crackle of the thunder, the thud of a hoof,
I like noise!

Amy Silvester (11)
Cottingham High School, Cottingham

Snug In My Bed!

It's morning
I'm snug in my bed
All cosy and snugly
Asleep in my bed

It's all icy outside
There's dew on the grass
But I don't really care
I'm snug in my bed

People are up
Getting ready for work
But I've got 10 more minutes
Being snug in my bed

I hear a loud voice in my head
Saying
'Wake up!
Wake up!'

I open my eyes to see
The lights shining brightly
The teacher babbling on
I'm not snug in my bed
I'm in boring old history!

Emily Hampson (12)
Cottingham High School, Cottingham

I Am Glad

I am glad to be going to watch Man Utd,
Walking on the path seeing the stadium,
Everyone wearing the red replica shirts,
Thousands of people queuing for tickets.

I am glad to be out of the house,
Away from school and books
And enjoying something different.

I hear the crowd shouting,
Man Utd are winning,
But then the football gets smacked
Right in my face,
Then I wonder who made that ball.

And I realised it was probably a small boy,
Who lives in a little lonely village,
Making hardly any money day after day.

And those little boys should be playing,
Laughing and running around,
But instead stand there each day,
For hardly any money while we kick the football around,
No thought for those little boys.

Daniel Shepherdson (12)
Cottingham High School, Cottingham

City Gent's Ideal Day

I woke up on a beach
Listening to the island breeze

With a Martini on one side
And fishing rod on the other

And the hot, golden sand
On the beach as far as the eye can see

People surfing on the waves
Toddlers with their nets in rock pools

I get a bite
And reel in with a tuna

And I can hear the roar of the sea
And smell the barbecue

But I always come through
I always come through

The roar of the sea is the roar of the cars
The smell of the barbecue is the smell of the fumes

It was all just a dream
Of me and someone on our honeymoon

The Martini is my grandad's teeth
In a pickle jar

I get myself a breakfast bar
And set off for work . . .

Another city day.

Michael Davidson (12)
Cottingham High School, Cottingham

Smoking

Don't put that stick in your mouth,
You'll never stop putting smoke out.
You'll huff and you'll puff,
Until you've had enough
And then you want another one after.

They're long, brown and white,
A real treat or delight,
If you like the Devil's stick.
You will realise you're tricked
And you'll never be able to get off them.

They'll fill your lungs with tar,
Scientists can collect it in jars,
You'll lose at least 10 years of your life,
Now isn't that a real delight?
Or you could die quicker with cancer.

They're bad for your health
And you'll lose lots of wealth.
With the white sticks
Your breath will just stink
And your teeth and fingers will go yellow.

So girls and boys,
Don't try the stick,
You'll regret it for life,
So do yourself a favour,
Don't smoke!

Josh Petterson (13)
Cottingham High School, Cottingham

Untitled

I'm home alone
And I'm starving
I go to the kitchen to get some food
I have a lot to choose from

I'm scoffing my face with goodies
When all of a sudden the news comes on
I listen quietly
People in different countries
Having nothing to eat

And here I am
Eating my way greedily through this food

I'm now daydreaming and thinking
What it would be like
To be starved, starved, starved

I stop eating my food
Those poor people with no food
And here I am saying
'I'm starving
I'm starving
I'm starving.'

Jessica Nettleton (12)
Cottingham High School, Cottingham

I Wake Up

The morning rises,
Calling of the wild birds,
Shining of the sparkling sun,
Wakes me up.

The calm blue waves,
Like a velvet blanket,
Crashing against the jagged rocks,
Wakes me up.

The long emerald grass,
Blows in the wind,
Its shadow looks like monsters,
Startled, I wake up.

Only to hear,
Beeping of car horns,
Ranting and raving voices,
Leaking of petrol.

Bumps here,
Bumps there,
Bumps everywhere.

Another dull city day.

Eve Goodby (12)
Cottingham High School, Cottingham

Attention Please!

We have just received some reports
That there is going to be some terrible weather
A tornado is coming
Please do not attempt to leave your shelter
Until you get given the all clear
If you do
Then you will be swept up
Into the air like leaves off a tree
The winds are as fast
As a rocket setting off to the moon
But please stay calm
And follow my instructions:
Firstly do not panic
Secondly go to your supermarket
And stock up on food if necessary
This tornado will not last long
You will have 10 minutes
To get to your nearest shelter
In 5 minutes
When I have finished this report
Your television will switch off
Then you will have 5 minutes
To get out of your house
And into your shelter
Please do not take any extra baggage
It will only take up more room
Please leave pets
Just remember
Some of us will be unlucky
Now please hurry to your shelter.

Emily Smith (14)
Cottingham High School, Cottingham

The Avalanche

Listen!
The radar is showing that somewhere,
Somewhere high in the mountains there's a
Very large snowball and at anytime it could fall;
Fall and crash to the ground!
So do what I say and don't panic!

No one should make any loud noise!
No one should jump around and make a thud!
No one should panic and
No one should break the rules!

Everyone shall tiptoe around!
Everyone shall turn off their music and televisions!
Everyone shall calm their children!
Everyone shall do what I say!
Now!

The radar is now showing
That the snowball is
Rocking - everyone stay calm
Swaying - stay as quiet as a mouse
Stopped - don't move
Falling

Stay calm! Stay calm!
New set of rules
Everyone (oh gosh, what shall I do?)
Stay calm (oh no, what shall I say?)
Don't panic (I'm panicking, I'm panicking)
Silence!
It's over!

Danielle Booth (13)
Cottingham High School, Cottingham

Attention Please!

We have received reports,
The wind is coming,
Be prepared, be prepared!
Tape up your windows,
Store in your food.
Be prepared, be prepared!
Move to safety,
Take your family,
Your local hospitals have been informed,
Your local shelters are preparing, just be prepared, be prepared!
The hurricanes are coming . . .
They've swept across the Atlantic,
They've hit the Caribbean,
They've wiped out precious lives,
Just be prepared, be prepared!
Leave your belongings,
After the forthcoming announcements,
Turn off your radio immediately,
Turn off your television now,
Wrap up warm, calm your family,
Now go, go quickly to your shelters.

Sara Parker (13)
Cottingham High School, Cottingham

The Colours Of My Imagination

There is a pit of lava,
A volcano,
With every shade of red.

There is a wave of camels,
A desert,
With every shade of yellow.

There is a cave of snakes,
A rainforest,
With every shade of green.

There is a sea of sharks,
An ocean,
With every shade of blue.

There is a puddle of mud,
A mountain,
With every shade of brown.

There is a river of colours,
A rainbow,
With every shade imaginable.

Josh Clarkson (12)
Cottingham High School, Cottingham

Attention Please!

Attention, attention please
Severe wind and rain is on the way.
The rain is beating down,
Like bullets being fired from a gun
And the wind howling
Like a pack of wolves.
So, lock your doors and
Try not to go out.
Just listen to my instructions
And please do not worry,
I will help you to get through the worst.
To start off make sure
All windows and doors are closed securely,
So no draught and rain can get in.
My next instruction is to get any blankets you have
Ready as morning will be cold and also will be night,
Everything will count,
Tuck small children into bed
And check them every so often.
Stock up all your tins of food,
Including water, this may not last long.
Finally, do not worry,
The rain and wind will not last long,
Now go and stay safe . . .

Sara Stewart (13)
Cottingham High School, Cottingham

Warning Poem

W hatever happened to all my friends
A nd my family?
R ed blood everywhere I look,
N ot many survivors,
 I wonder what happened to the survivors?
N o one anywhere I look,
G od, help me.

O h God, it's horrible, they're all gone,
F riends, family, everyone.

N o survivors . . .
U sing the farmland I have to live,
C racked land beneath my feet,
L ots of corpses everywhere I look,
E arth is dying,
A PCs carrying the few soldiers that are alive,
R emembering my family and friends.

A nd still I cry for my friends and family,
T his is it, I'm all alone,
T he end is near.
A men, I hope I live through this
C ans of tinned food, all I have to eat,
K egs of water, all I have left to drink.

James Filby (13)
Cottingham High School, Cottingham

Anger Is Only One Letter Short Of Danger

She knew it was there,
She couldn't get rid of it,
Wherever she went,
Wherever she ran,
She knew she could never hide from it.
Twisting through her veins,
Like snakes with their venom,
Never-ending snakes, always holding her back.
The worst part is that you can't see it,
You can only *feel* it, *feel* the pain.
She was told once that it had gone and she was happy,
But it came back after her again and although she could not see it,
She could see the effect working its way to the surface,
The effect of trying to get it away from her.
She would always ask, 'Why me?'
Finally one night, whilst she was sleeping, it got her,
She didn't make a sound.
No one knew.
No one also knew that she tried to kill herself, to try to prevent it.
But it got her in the end.
Just like that, she went.
It got her. Got her. Got her in the end.
Didn't stand a chance.
Got her, one night, got her.

The cancer.

Roxanne Bedforth (16)
Cottingham High School, Cottingham

Tornado Coming

We interrupt your programme to
Inform you that in twenty minutes
A tornado has been predicted
To arrive in Hull
You must leave, head north
If evacuation is not possible
Seek shelter underground
Or in a secure room with no windows
Do not try to save loved ones
Odds are, they are evacuating the city too
If after the tornado
You find yourself trapped
Cry for help and there is
A great chance you will be found
If you hear somebody
Shout for help
After the disaster notify the services
Immediately
Run for your life, seek safety
This warning has come
To an end.

Callum Shields (13)
Cottingham High School, Cottingham

A Lesson Learnt

It never even crossed her mind
That it might happen to them
It only happens to others you see
People on TV
And a couple of people at school
But not us, not *her* family

People don't die till they're old you see . . .
Until they're warm and safe in their beds
They drift off peacefully in their sleep
And they don't ever suffer

She told herself that from when she was very small
She realised it was naïve
But that way she never had to worry you see . . .
She would always be looked after because the people *she* loved
Would never be taken away
Not for a long, long time

She learnt just how wrong she was that day
The nineteenth of January last year
He was only 39 you see . . . that's far too young to die
She could never have imagined that
Her dad - the biggest, bravest man she knew would be stolen
So suddenly

And she would be left
With a huge chunk missing from her life
And a whole lot of regrets
Why did she never tell him she loved him?
Why didn't she appreciate him enough?
It's too late now
She learnt her lesson.

Holly Dick (16)
Cottingham High School, Cottingham

Warnings Of Fire

It may be fun
With its dancing flame,
Colours like red and yellow
And blue flames.
Sparks
Like stars painted on a black canvas,
Sparkling
Like fairy lights.
It may be fun at first
Until it burns.
A destroyer
Don't get too close.
Flame flaring, pretty
Until it bites down,
Forests, trees taken by the thousand.
Houses, a full city at once!
People, fire can kill!
It may be fun
And pretty
With its dancing
Multicoloured flames.
Oh, it may be
A delight to watch
But it burns
It destroys, kills.
Just stay safe
Don't play with fire.

Felicity Hill (13)
Cottingham High School, Cottingham

My Bottom Drawer

My bottom drawer
Is full of magical things
Little dresses I used to wear
With pretty pink frilly rims

A pair of cute cotton booties
My tiny rocking chair
Very special photographs
Wrapped with real leopard fur

A lovely raggy teddy
A little pinkie ring
An old chewed-up cat toy
A plastic crown for a king

When I'm even older
I'm going to have even more
And browse upon all the wonders
Of my wondrous bottom drawer.

Rebecca Tindall (11)
Cottingham High School, Cottingham

Lots Of Things

I like lots of things . . .
The aliens from Mars, the shell of a turtle
The sound of a telly on a stand
The beach at Brid, the waves of the sea
The windows of a house as it lights up on the night
The nest of birds, the tongue of a frog
The tower of a wonderful place
The school of lessons, the head of a horse
The glory of a team winning
The books of Harry Potter, the hair of a dog
The world of everything,
I like lots of things.

Daniel Richardson (11)
Cottingham High School, Cottingham

I Am . . .

I am the day
I am the night
I am the fire that burns ever bright

I am the child
I am the mother
I am the one that makes people suffer

I am the friend
I am the foe
I am the knowledge people strive to know

I am the lover
I am the touch
I am the one you'll miss so much

I am all of these things that make life spin
Yet I can't decide where I begin.

Clare Humblestone (16)
Cottingham High School, Cottingham

The Thin Line Between Love And Hate

Two things, two emotions, so far apart, yet so close,
How the things we love and cherish,
Become the things we loathe and hate,
With just one single action, one word, one gesture,
Hope can turn to despair, love to hate.

Trust is a fool's term, those led astray only to find betrayal,
The people we trust, we think we do,
To trust empowers them, so they can stab you in the back,
Trust flourishes in the minds of the weak and destroys them,
Trust can turn to betrayal, love to hate.

Love describes weakness, a mind finding something,
Someone to cling to, something to keep you alive,
But why? In the end we all know nothing can last,
One simple obstacle, the mind stumbles,
Love turns to despair.

Phillip Vine (15)
Cottingham High School, Cottingham

Untitled

The sun sets down beyond the horizon
The black cloak covers the streets like a sheet covering a bed
The street lights come on
And the stars begin to twinkle

I'm walking alone down a street filled with darkness
Lonely, cold and aware of every noise that's being made
Every rattle, scratch, bang, even squeak, everything
My senses are heightened
Looking around like a keen owl's eye

I'm walking alone down a street filled with darkness
Just walking, straight forward into the darkness and for evermore
With only the street lights and the stars to guide me
What to do but keep walking?
Where to? Just keep walking until I find somewhere recognisable
Home, shops, anywhere, as long as I find somewhere I know
Somewhere safe

I'm walking alone down a street filled with darkness
Suddenly the street lights stop, I carry on walking
Now eyes wider than before
Walking into the unknown, with only the stars to guide me
I carry on walking cautiously
Where am I?
I don't know
Do you?

Anthony Knight (10)
Cottingham High School, Cottingham

My Family And Me

My mum is going out to work,
My dad has got a gun,
My brother's in a mood again,
I'm sure he's going to run.

My cousin's coming round today,
Although the house is such a tip.
My mum and dad are going mad,
They're surely going to flip.

My auntie is playing with matches,
My uncle's going mad,
But actually to tell the truth,
My family aren't that bad.

What a weird old family,
What a funny lot,
Sometimes I think I'm
The only sane one they've got.

Amy Ward (11)
Cottingham High School, Cottingham

The School

A school is boring
A school is great
A school is the place where you find a mate!

A school has lessons
A school has a hall
A school has a disco with a disco ball!

A school is big
A school has a gate
A school is the place where you come in late!

Jordan Lea (11)
Oaklands School, York

My Sonnet

Shall I compare Jon to a summer's day?
Thou art more excited and more happy,
His temper, like storms, comes quick - doesn't stay,
He's my brother, mad, jolly, my chappy,
Sometimes too hot the eye of Heaven shines,
His hair is more orange than a sunset.
He has travelled further than River Tyne,
I have known him forever, he's no pet.
But thou's love and passion will not leave him,
Nor shall he lose the world he has known well,
Nor shall he forget his family and Kim,
When his house and belongings go and sell,
So long as you can see and hear, you know
As long as you live, you will be loved so . . .

Kimberley Walker (13)
Oaklands School, York

Friends!

(A Sonnet)

Shall I compare friends to a summer's day?
Friends are reliable and loads of fun
Sometimes the sun is too hot to go play
I can go out once my homework is done
It is so boring to be on your own
It is much better to have company
I love to talk to friends over the phone
I love it when my friends come to see me
Friends are always there when you are in need
We love to have a chat and lounge about
My friends don't have any hatred or greed
But sometimes we all have to scream and shout
A real friend is someone who does these things
Happy as the sun that the morning brings.

Kerry Fong (13)
Oaklands School, York

Animals Give Joy As A Summer's Day

Animals give joy as a summer's day
They are so much more caring and funny
So sweet and so jumpy that I might say
They make me feel so warm and so sunny

Animals can hide in fear or fright
Just be quiet and you will see them play
With warmth for the day, for the sky there's light
Oh how pretty just like a summer's day

Animals will be with us forever
So please care for them till the very end
And let's all try to work hard together
To stop animals being hunted or penned

Baby animals are born in springtime
In winter some hibernate such as bats
Though birds like swallows fly south in a line
But some stay here all seasons like cats

They make me feel so happy that I say
Animals give joy as a summer's day.

Vanessa-Marie Lowth (13)
Oaklands School, York

The Castle

The castle is big,
The castle is tall,
The castle is the place with a scary hall.

The castle is cold,
The castle is old,
The castle is the place with hidden gold.

The castle is empty,
It's got a broken door,
The castle has a carpet on the creaky floor.

Ryan Taylor (11)
Oaklands School, York

TV
(A Sonnet)

I'll compare TV to a summer's day,
Thou art more shinier and so more square,
It's so precise to me, that's what I say,
It plays all of my best programmes with care.
Sometimes too hot, the eye of Heaven shines,
So you're trapped inside the house by yourself,
Even though time and day always declines,
The TV will always be on your shelf,
But the TV's shine shall not ever fade,
Or it shall not lose all its great action,
It will not lay still in the gloomy shade,
When it's there for your own satisfaction,
So long as we can breathe or eyes can see,
So long lives TV, this gives life to me.

Jessica Ingleby (13)
Oaklands School, York

My Sonnet

Shall I compare Bob to a summer's day?
He is art more cheeky, funny and sweet,
Runs about and scares the people away,
Guarding your gardens all through the warm heat,
Sometimes too hot the eye of Heaven shines,
Hair is as brown as a small dark brown log,
Been further than Newcastle-upon-Tyne
And has a toy that's as green as a frog.
But thy eternal happiness shan't fade,
Nor shall he feel sadness every day,
Nor shall he forget his world that God made,
When the spring blossoms start to bloom in May.
So long as he can see and hear, you know,
As long as you live, he will be loved so.

Louise Railton (13)
Oaklands School, York

My Poem

Shall I compare football to a summer's day?
A football is more exciting and fun,
If we don't play at home, we play away,
We don't like playing in the blinding sun,
Sometimes the referee is unfair,
Sometimes the linesman makes wrong decisions,
You can watch the match on television,
You can play football mostly anywhere,
You can be a ref, sub or a player,
To stay extra fit eat fruit such as pears,
If it's cold when you play wear two layers,
Keep in mind football's a great game to play,
It will remain the best game to this day.

Callie Potter (13)
Oaklands School, York

Shall I . . . ?

Shall I compare leprechauns to a summer's day?
Thou art more rebellious and silly,
Chases and scares all those people away,
When entered the room they make you chilly.
Sometimes too great the greenness of them shine,
But often the colour of them are dimmed,
Just like this sonnet they too speak in rhyme,
Their toenails are always gonna be trimmed.
But thy eternal mischief shall not fade,
Nor lose possession of that unfair tone,
Nor will they try to fix all the mess made,
They'll take it too far and on they will drone,
So long as we can see and we can hear,
The little green leprechauns will appear!

Kirsty Hill (13)
Oaklands School, York

Seasons Haikus

Spring
Flowers are growing
The children come out to play
Parents are happy

Summer
The sun is shining
Suntans appear on people
Everybody's warm

Autumn
Leaves fall off trees
Playing children jump in leaves
It starts to get cold

Winter
The snow starts to fall
Father Christmas is coming
Everyone's happy.

Leanne Deighton (11)
Oaklands School, York

Good Advice

Across the lonely moors it crept
Whilst the world about it slept
Dreaming of a sunnier day
Into which it did not stray
The moors were beautiful, but deadly too
Into it, no bird flew
It was heavy, it was vast
Many days it did last
Into it you must not stray
For surely you will lose your way
Mist is clearly, obviously 'it'
And though it clears, bit by bit
Don't go through alone, please understand -
Take somebody else and hold their hand.

Amber Wardley (12)
Oaklands School, York

The Golden Eagle

She flies through the silvery sky
With a golden twinkle in her eye
Flying to her nest
She never takes a rest
Feeding her young
With all her fun

Flying high she glides over the sea
The children can't yet be so free
They are flying way behind
Can they find
Their mother in time
Before they hand in a big space of crime?

Suddenly their mother sweeps and shines
To save her children one last time
She flies through the sunlight
Trying to put up with the fight
Her children go alone
Their mother had already shone.

Rebecca Heath (11)
Oaklands School, York

Why?

Mum, why is there potato in my mash?
Why isn't the moon made out of cheese?
Why is the rain wet?
Why is the sky blue?
Why is the grass green?
Why is snow sometimes yellow?
Why isn't there any toad in my hole?
Why do I have to go to bed when I'm not tired?
Why do I have to get up when I am?
Why do clouds look like candyfloss but you can't eat them?
Why do I have to eat my broccoli? I don't like eating trees!
Mum, what does why mean?

Rachael Vardy (12)
Oaklands School, York

A Load O' Nonsense

I can't think what to write about,
So I'll write a load o' nonsense,
It could be a forest,
But that would be far too dense!

I thought perhaps a wizard,
Or maybe the ocean blue,
But then I thought of cowboys
Or maybe even you!

A butterfly, so pretty,
An aircraft in the sky,
The crunch of autumn leaves,
Or fireworks flying high?

Finally I chose this,
I hope that it makes sense,
Cos I decided to write down,
A good old load o' nonsense!

Amy Thompson (12)
Oaklands School, York

Hallowe'en

H is for hairy, big hairy monsters
A is for Amber who is holding the party
L is for late, the party will end late
L is for lanterns, I'll carry them around
O is for October, the month that it is in
W is for werewolf, I might dress up as one
E is for eerie, the night might be eerie
E is for exorcist, we might need one of those
N is for nougat, I don't want any of that.

Julia Hudson (12)
Oaklands School, York

Basketball

Shall I compare basketball to a summer's day?
This game is more exciting and more street
You have to be a gangster to come and play
And dribble the ball like a hip hop beat

My favourite play is the ale hoop
I love the shots that make the net go swish
You better not be in the losing group
By chance or by skill to win is my wish

Be embarrassed when I cross you over
'Cause my skill will make the cheerleaders sing
You better be looking for a four-leaf clover
'Cause you're playing seven-foot six Yau Ming

So now I know I am king of the court
No one can beat me, not even Hot Sauce.

Ross Lancaster (13)
Oaklands School, York

Ross

(A Sonnet)

Shall I compare Ross to a summer's day?
Thou art more gangster nor more a ginner
He's really cool in his own sort of way
Never a loser, always a winner
And take my advice, never mess with Ross
He might not like you, he might give a scream
You spoil his wish and you will die because
To play in the NBA, that's his dream
He likes a bit of a flirt with the girls
But there's nowt wrong with that, good on ya lad
He once grew his hair, it went into curls
It looked quite alright, it wasn't that bad
So as I told you, never mess with Ross
Cos I can assure you, he is the boss!

Arron Fishwick (13)
Oaklands School, York

Wake Up!

Wake up, I can't be late
I can't be bothered, they'll have to wait
I pull the covers over my face
All with a quick and thorough pace
Wake up, I can't be late!

Wake up, I can't be late
I can't be bothered, they'll have to wait
I see the clock
Disturbed by a knock
Wake up, I can't be late!

Wake up, I can't be late
I can't be bothered, they'll have to wait
My sister crawls in
She roots in the bin
Wake up, I can't be late!

Wake up, I can't be late
I can't be bothered, they'll have to wait
I finally decide
Not to hide
And shake the sleep from my eyes.

Gemma Moore (11)
Oaklands School, York

Leaving

I've just found out it's great
But wait you say, you're going somewhere else
Uh-oh!

Two friends with me
The rest have gone and scarpered
It won't be the same again
Uh-oh!

Three friends, including me
They might pick each other
And I will be left out
Uh-oh!

So maybe if we do the same languages
We can be partners
You're doing the same languages as her
Uh-oh!

Well at break we can hang out
In our special group of three
'OK,' they say

Great!

Elaine Hannigan (12)
Oaklands School, York

The Midnight Swordsman

He rides through the forest,
With a heart as black as sin,
His horse is strong and muscle-bound,
While he is gaunt and thin,
He is the midnight swordsman
And his story is lost to time,
Yet all who live nearby,
Know of his terrible crimes,
But what black deeds has he committed?
To be punished in this way,
Made to walk forever,
Throughout night and day.
He has tortured many a man
And killed, some say, many more

His tortured spirit must hunt . . .
For the blood of the pure!
For his terrible hunger,
This is the only cure!
Now he haunts the forest,
Until the end of all,
Where he'll fall to Hell's icy grip,
But never Heaven's call.
All who venture here
Are fools of the highest order!
Never enter the forest,
For *he* haunts that border
And if you go there on a stormy night,
You'll hear him riding in the glade,
Hurrying to the embrace of shadow,
Blood flecked on his blade . . .

Corey Soper (12)
Oaklands School, York

The Mighty Samurai

The silver sword that's in his hand
Glistens in his eye
Is this bloodthirsty warrior
The mighty samurai?

He fastens up his armour
He sharpens his steel blade
The emperor's majestic army
Is ready to invade

He seeks the shogun warlord
And shoots him with his bow
And using his katana
He casts the fatal blow

He is a true born killer
He slaughters all that stand
It's true, this mighty samurai
Is known throughout the land

But they have lost the battle
And he is left alive
He would rather lose his life
Than surrender and survive

The ancient samurai customs are honour, glory and pride
So the only thing left for the swordsman
Is to commit ritual suicide

On the ground he lay lifeless
It was his choice to die
This is the final resting place
Of the mighty samurai.

Connor Rowbotham (12)
Oaklands School, York

On The Road We Go!

On the road we go,
On the road we go,
Singing a song,
Let off a pong,
On the road we go.

Up the hill we go,
Up the hill we go,
The headlight fell out,
We wandered about,
Up the hill we go.

Through the village we go,
Through the village we go,
We saw a truck,
The driver had a funny look,
Through the village we go.

To the seaside we go,
To the seaside we go,
We got stuck,
In a big pile of muck,
Back home we go!

Darryl Rae (12)
Oaklands School, York

The Ballad Of Love

The ballad of love,
Tells a simple little tale,
The love of a dove
And the love of a quail.

It all started off
At a party parade,
The quail saw the dove
And bought her lemonade.

The dove sat next to the quail,
She said, 'Thank you very much.'
On her other side sat a snail,
She invited him home for lunch

And ever since that day,
True love has blossomed for them,
They've always been okay,
With a baby boy called Chem.

The ballad of love,
The ballad of love,
Two different types,
Having found love!

Arielle Redman (12)
Oaklands School, York

The Effects Of War

'Aarrgghh,' screeched a voice
'Help,' cried another
Do we have a choice?

A child sobbing
A mother dying
An evil voice laughed

Aaaarrrrgggghhhh!

Silence!

Disaster!

'Never again,' said a muffled voice
The voice was a girl
'This my friends is the effects of war,'
The girl choked, all tense
Then she relaxed, her last breath slowly drew away.

Claire Nesfield (12)
Oaklands School, York

What Is It?

What is it? It's big and hairy.
What is it? It's mean and scary!

What is it? It's tall and fat.
What is it? Its chest is flat!

What is it? It's coming closer.
What is it? It's not a her!

What is it? It's violent and horrid.
What is it? It's not named Syd!

What is it? It's ugly and weird.
What is it? I've always feared!

What is it? It's old and bad.
Oh my God, it is my dad!

Robyn Carter (12)
Oaklands School, York

The Zoo

A is for alligator that snaps its teeth and groans,
B is for grizzly bear which always growls and moans,
C is for camel which usually has a hump,
D is for dog which always makes me jump,
E is for eagle which has a long sight,
F is for fox which comes out at night,
G is for gorilla which has a mighty thud,
H is for hippo which slaps around in the mud,
I is for ibex which eats mountain plants,
J is for jellyfish which lights up like a lamp,
K is for kingfisher which flies across the river,
L is for lion which eats a zebra's liver,
M is for monkey which is cheeky all the time,
N is for nanny goat which could chew a washing line,
O is for an ostrich which runs across the sand,
P is for piranha which will bite off your hand,
Q is for queen bee which has a horrible sting,
R is for robin which can beautifully sing,
S is for snake which slithers and frights,
T is for a tiger which always roars and bites,
U is for a unicorn which sparkles day and night,
V is for a vulture which circles out of sight,
W is for a weasel which eats lots of mice,
X is for extinct, killed off by the ice,
Y is for yak, its coat is rather coarse,
Z is for zebra, it is like a stripy horse.

Tim Street (12)
Oaklands School, York

A Day To Remember

A day to remember
Is the 11th September,
Where the trade towers collapsed in two,
A day to remember
Is the 11th September,
People inside didn't know what to do.

The firemen rushed inside,
Whilst families watched and cried,
They saved as many people as they could,
The firemen rushed inside,
Whilst families watched and cried,
All that was left was gravel and blood.

A day to remember
Is the 11th September,
Where the trade towers collapsed in two,
A day to remember
Is the 11th September,
The year before 2002.

Katie Friend (12)
Oaklands School, York

Lauren

L oopy and lazy, my friends call me crazy
A dmiring the art then I'm ready to start
U nder the covers bullying my brothers
R eading a book, on my homework I'm stuck
E ntering the Internet, leaving the teaching train
N utty as a butty, dangerous and daring
    I'm a girl on a mission and destined to kill.

Lauren Blount (11)
Oaklands School, York

A New School

I enter what they so-called 'school'
I must have been the only one
To try and attempt the times of the past
It's all quiet
Its master-classes suck you up like a hoover
Scraping across the newly-laid floor
Suddenly a screech
Like a train whistle sounding like it's coming towards me
Belting out loudly
I am no longer alone
Giants tread on me like I'm a part of the ground
Such a noise, a deafening sound of torture
Touches my soul like a whip lashing on my back
Then I hear that screeching again
Everyone, everything dissolves with a flash of my own eyes
Was I dreaming? Was I? Or was I?
'Here you are!' calls a distant sound
'My friend,' I sobbed
A sudden whisper from behind crackled
Then I too vanished
Like them before me
That was just the beginning of my new school.

Sophie Scaife (11)
Oaklands School, York

Just A Poem

This could be a poem about I don't know what,
Could be about climates cold or hot
. . . It's not

It could be about friendship, hate or love
Could be about animals, hamster or dove
. . . It's not

It could be about music, why not say 'Busted?'
Could be about friends, how much they're trusted
. . . It's not

It could be about hobbies, sports I like
Could be about technology - the exercise bike!
. . . It's not

It could be about subjects - take art for example
Could be about shopping, or a free sample!
. . . It's not

This poem is made to fill in time
The secret is to make it rhyme
. . . It has!

Laura O'Donovan (12)
Oaklands School, York

What's The Time?

Mum, Mum, what time is it?
Mum, please tell me the time,
Mum, Mum, what time is it?
Tell me, it isn't a crime.

Mum, Mum, what time is it?
Is it nearly time for tea?
Mum, Mum, what time is it?
Come on Mum, please tell me.

Mum, Mum, what time is it?
Is it time to play with my toys?
Mum, Mum, what time is it?
Tell me and I'll stop making this noise.

Mum, Mum, what time is it?
Oh no, it isn't time for bed
Mum, Mum, what time is it?
Don't listen to what I just said.

Joanne Burton (12)
Oaklands School, York

Listen

Listen: the Morse Code of a woodpecker
            the screaming of a tree
            the deep and dark breathing
            of the inner child in me

Listen: the gossip of a flower
            the whisper in the air
            the sound of a grubby hand
            combing through its hair

Listen: the click of a light switch
            in my English class
            the sound of a twitch
            in a piece of glass

Listen: the rustle of paper
            the scratch of a pen
            the sound of band practice
            with my brother, Ben.

Katie Janes (12)
Oaklands School, York

Midnight Murder

She lay still on the floor
Her blood on the open door
The knife lay in the next room
Next to the blood-handled broom

Laying there she tried to think back
To the attacker all dressed in black
She remembered the cold knife slid into her back
He had attacked her from the back

She had crawled into the other room
And tried to steady herself near the broom
As she lay there blood flowed
It seemed to release a load

Her eyes slowly closed to darkness
And she saw less and less
As her heart stopped beating
The attacker started fleeing.

Jasmine Cuinu (12)
Oaklands School, York

The Hideaway

There she is in a darkened room
She sits there quietly waiting
In her own little tomb
She can't hear the arguments from below
But she knows that they are there
She is breathing heavily but slow

As she steps out into the light
She hears the door slamming
'He'll come home,' she mutters, hoping she is right
The next thing she hears is her mum crying
She is talking on the phone
Saying something about the girl's dad lying

Four long days pass and he's still not back
She knows where he is staying
In the woods, in a shack
He usually rings by now
To say he's coming home
Although she doesn't know how

Her mum asked to talk to her
She thought it would be good
'I'm sorry,' her mum said in a whisper
'Your dad won't be coming home this time'
After a while her mum remarried
Her dad went to jail for doing a dreadful crime.

Nicola Hartley (13)
Oaklands School, York

Winter

Winter is so cold,
There is no way to escape it,
And then the rain comes down,
Winter is too cold.

All the children wear hats
And their big fluffy coats,
All their ears are red,
Winter is too cold.

The adults sit in their cars,
Waiting for it to warm up,
You see the look on their faces,
You see the children laugh,
Winter is too cold.

You get to school
And your teacher's been snowed in,
So you're stuck with a supply all day,
Winter is too cold.

It's break time
And everyone's too cold to move,
Winter is too cold,
Winter is too cold.

Matthew Orme (12)
Oaklands School, York

Our Dog, Trigger

Have you ever owned a boxer?
Well, just think twice before you do,
They're clumsy and they dribble,
Plus they slobber over you!

They'll chew almost anything,
From shoes to dining tables
And as soon as you're not looking,
They chew the telly cables.

We called our dog Trigger
And my dad shouts, 'He's got to go!'
As he tears around the garden,
With the washing line in tow.

We go to Gran and Grandad's
On a Sunday for our lunch
And we have to take our Trigger,
For his lamb and Yorkshire munch.

My grandad's got some wellies,
He tries very hard to hide,
But Trigger always finds them,
Which comes as no surprise.

We love our Trigger dearly
And Trigger's here to keep,
He's cheeky and he's naughty,
But good when he's asleep.

Claire Hebblethwaite (12)
Oaklands School, York

I Want You To Go To School, Son

(Based on 'I Don't Want To Go To School, Mum' by Pam Ayres)

I want you to go to school now, Son
It's nearly half-past eight
Come on, get your coat on, Son
Or else you're gonna be late

I know you don't want to go now, Son
But you're getting under my feet
I need to do the washing dear, Son
Come on, get in the car seat

We'll be there soon, Son
I'll be free of you at last
I know that sounds mean, Son
But you've never done it in the past

Just shut up now, Son
I really need to be free
Come on, walk faster, Son
I need a cup of tea

I'm nearly shot of you now, Son
Under two minutes to go
Stop being silly now, Son
But there goes the bell and off you go.

Rachel Noble (13)
Oaklands School, York

Iraq Wars Ruin My Life!

I work round big buildings under the rain,
Gives me money but gives me pain!
It's hard to smile where I live in Iraq,
For war is upon this place's trembling back!
Suddenly . . . *bang, smash, tumble, smack*,
I'm on the floor, it goes pitch-black!
Terror is brought to my hearing and eyes,
For all I can hear is shouting and cries!
I'm stuck under everything, I can see only black,
There's rocks falling on me, nearly breaking my back!
I'm screaming and shouting but no one will come,
I'm stuck with the frightening darkness where there is no sun!
The whispers of ghostly suffering,
The screaming is from the weak ones that echo down the darkness,
Will I ever see the light again . . . who knows?
'What's going to happen to me?' I say
As I feel a heartless shiver down my spine!

Kirsty Bennett (12)
Oaklands School, York

My New Puppy

I wake up and go downstairs,
To feel the warmth of her silky coat,
She sits there with her head tilted to one side,
The deep blue gaze of her eyes
And her frantically wagging, stumpy tail.

When I get home from school,
She's waiting at the front door,
I pat her softly on the head,
I teach her to fetch a toy.

Her name is Wisp, the cutest puppy in the universe,
But not for long, she'll soon grow up.

Emily Walden (11)
Ripon Grammar School, Ripon

Never Enough

It's never good enough is it?
Could be better couldn't it?
I could've tried harder couldn't I?
You seem to find
That it's so easy for me.
You have no clue.
It's harder than you could ever imagine.
Every day is a struggle.
It's my dream that I'm killing,
So at least give a shoulder.
A shoulder to cry on,
Which I can always rely on,
No matter how good or bad I do.
No matter how much I seem to disappoint you.
You think I can push myself further.
Well, any further and I'm gone.
The edge of this cliff is at my feet.
If I fall I know you'll be upset
That I didn't try harder.
Didn't do better.
Well, I've had it.
No more trying to please you.
No more waiting for you.
I wanted you to say you were proud.
You didn't, so forget it.
I don't need your approval.
I have mine
And it's all that matters.

Rafa Alam (17)
Ripon Grammar School, Ripon

Cycling

Cycling is my favourite sport
You don't know what it's like

To cycle from port to port
In a foreign land

Carrying all your own kit
In two hefty panniers

Speeding down the side of a valley
Then up the other side

Going up the hills
And discovering a remote café

Going down the hill
When you are full of tea

Going on the group rides
And leaving them all behind

Getting back and drinking hot chocolate
In front of the TV.

Richard Delf (11)
Ripon Grammar School, Ripon

What Is Fear?

Is fear the shadow man creeping around?
Is it ghouls that make no sound?
Is fear a war between good and evil
That burrows deep just like a weevil?

Is fear the sound of hissing snakes
Or is it the sound that a roaring bear makes?
Is fear the lashing of the evil man's whips
Or is it a death hound with bloodstained lips?

Is fear the moment when the clock strikes midnight
Or the start of a nightmare with no end in sight?
Is fear the time when nobody cares
Or is fear the time when you die unawares?

James Simmons (11)
Ripon Grammar School, Ripon

Horses

Black, brown, grey or white,
These can stay out all night.
Pony nuts, hay or grass,
They can get a very big mass.

Synthetic or leather,
To them it weighs no more than a feather.
Cottage craft or French link,
The thing is, they are not pink.

Knee-length or jodhpur boots,
Put them on and off she shoots.
Hats can be covered or bare,
But they still protect heads and hair.

You can canter to jump,
Though when you do it, don't give her a bump.
Out hacking can be fun,
Unless you're caught with a gun.

Rachael Sharp (11)
Ripon Grammar School, Ripon

Jungle

The lonely wind howls
through the whispering trees.
All night long the water falls
smashing against the rocks.
I look up to the sky
the silver stars look vibrant
against the coal-black sky.

Cold drops of water
burn my face,
like the spherical ball of fire
that lights up our sky
and all the beauty of the world,
especially the jungles.

Georgina Burnett (11)
Ripon Grammar School, Ripon

Go For Gold

Shining bright in the dark night sky,
Proud above the stade,
The beacon of light, the Olympic flame,
Lightens the parade.

The best celebration of sport,
With athletes from all over the world,
Who gather beneath the torch,
Their national colours unfurled.

The training and commitment,
Pays off at last,
When standing on the podium,
Your flag upon the mast.

Realising your dreams,
As shining futures dawn,
Champions come and go,
And new stars are born.

Winning isn't easy,
You've got to be real bold,
So go for it, get there,
Come on, go for gold!

Gabriella Ireland (15)
Ripon Grammar School, Ripon

Murder!

Creak, crash, smash,
I hear a noise in the dead of night.
Whish, whoosh, whoo,
I feel a chill in the dead of night.
Dark, evil, silent,
I see a shadow in the dead of night.
Creak, crash, smash, whish, whoosh, whoo, *bang!*
I fall to the floor in the dead of night.

Sally Jones (11)
Ripon Grammar School, Ripon

Seasons

The cherry tree blossoms in the spring,
As the thrush begins to sing.
The snow has gone and the rivers are flowing,
The grass is green and the sun is glowing.
Christmas has gone and Easter is coming,
The children play whilst the bees are humming.

Hello summer the swallows abound,
Dipping low and flying around.
Trips to the seaside, waves hit the shores,
Climbing up trees and playing outdoors.
Pollen that floats around in the air,
The sun on my face and a breeze in my hair.

Oh that autumn, close the door,
The wind blows up underneath the floor.
A sea of yellow, a carpet of gold,
The leaves change colour as they grow old.
Harvest festival is coming soon,
The crops grow ripe as the apples bloom.

Winter brings a wind that bites,
Short, short days and long, long nights.
Wrapped up warm against the chill,
Is that ice on my window sill.
Footprint patterns in the snow,
They're oh so pretty but soon they'll go.

The seasons pass by one by one,
The cycle goes on and on.
Never will the seasons stop,
They keep on going round the block.
Some are cold and some are hot,
That's why I like seasons a lot.

Danielle Graham (12)
Ripon Grammar School, Ripon

Alone

People are all out for money
No one ever wants to lend a helping hand
No one cares for the fellow man
If everyone would just give
Then everyone would be able to live
In peace and perfect harmony
No one cares
All the families in despair
And the government doesn't do anything
Anything to help them out
To set an example
Watch all the children die
From hunger and the common cold
Cruelty
Of humanity
Change is in order
We can't do it alone.

Paul Midgley (16)
Ripon Grammar School, Ripon

Just Think

Just think for a minute how lucky you are,
A roof over your head and even a car:
You're relatively rich; owning gold
While others suffer in the cold.

Some people ask for more and more:
They just don't care for the poor.
Spare a thought for those in need,
Don't fill yourself with awful greed.

You should be thankful for what you've got:
Don't ask for more, you've got a lot!
There are others less fortunate than you,
So be happy with what you have and do.

Adam Robinson (11)
Ripon Grammar School, Ripon

When I Am Older

When I am older,
I am going to be,
The greatest pilot,
You'll ever see.

I'll fly a fighter jet,
The best you can get.

When I am older,
I'm going to become,
The best maths teacher,
That can do *any* sum.

I'll teach a class
And all their tests they will pass.

When I am older,
I'm going to work,
As an undercover detective
And in corners I'll lurk.

I'll solve mysteries
And find out criminals' histories.

When I am older,
I'll end up,
As a top surgeon,
Doing a major op.

I'll do transplants,
For people with bad parts,
Like lungs, livers, kidneys and hearts.

Whatever I'll be,
I'm going to be great,
No, greater than great.
You'll see!

Natalie Turner (11)
Ripon Grammar School, Ripon

The Snake

The dry, dusty desert sand blew across the rocks,
Long green blades of grass rustled in the wind,
Palm trees bowed their luscious leaves
And through the sand, a snake slithered,
Like a twisting, coiling rope,
It edged along the ground.

A face compared with Satan,
Stares at you, daring you closer,
If you run, it will follow,
If you hide, it will seek,
But if you stay, it will kill.

Its body is dappled with exotic patterns,
Warning you to stay away,
A quiet hiss, a milky-eyed stare
And fangs like arrows, tipped with poison
Are the only warnings you receive,
Before it closes in.

The snake is weaving through the sand,
Gliding silently in your footsteps,
A sharp pain in your leg,
You fall to the sandy ground in agony,
Sweat covers your forehead.

The venom courses through your veins,
You die slowly, bewildered and confused
And the snake, like a ghost, slides past,
Towards the dusty horizon.

Giles Pitts (12)
Ripon Grammar School, Ripon

Seasons

S pring is full of wonderful things
P resent are daffodils in the sun
R ainbows are shining in the sky
I nteracting with the heavens
N ewborn lambs are born
G rowing through the year

S ummer is the time of warmth
U sing the sun while we can
M aybe we'll have a good time
M aybe we won't
E njoying the holidays
R emembering the summer thoughts

A lways playing outside
U ntil the autumn comes
T hen we are inside
U ndercover, wrapped up warm
M aking cakes, baking buns
N ever forgetting the time when autumn comes

W inter is the weather champion
I nternational coldness
N earing to Christmas time
T insel, glitter, sparkle squares
E vergreen trees, but mostly bareness
R emember now the seasons that have passed.

Ella Stelling (11)
Ripon Grammar School, Ripon

Chocoholic

One day in town I stopped and stared
At the biggest ever éclair,
The chocolate so smooth and brown,
So tasty, it's never caused a frown.

I walked inside this special shop,
I glanced around and then I stopped,
Delicious bars jumping out with glee,
'Can I help you?' an assistant said to me.

I'm doing fine,
I'm up on cloud nine,
But it's so hard to choose,
I'm going for a Bluez!

I undo the coil
And rip open the foil,
I'm starting to dribble,
I take a nibble.

Perfect!

Alex Warriner (11)
Ripon Grammar School, Ripon

The Snail

The snail is quite amazing,
Walking up the wall.
It slides and slips very slowly,
Going for a crawl.

Its slimy tail winds its way,
Round and round the path.
Up through the window
And into the bath.

Its hard brown shell is curvy,
With a hole in the side,
It follows the snail all the time,
With every slippery stride.

Robin Whitfield (11)
Ripon Grammar School, Ripon

Confusion

Yesterday today was tomorrow
And tomorrow, today will be gone
This is not a thought to bring about sorrow
But just a fact to ponder on

Maybe tomorrow, today will be
Just a dream that was dreamt yesterday
And today today's dream was able to see
Ideas that were stored away

Perhaps in a year or so to come
Yesterday, today and tomorrow
Will have had their fair share of sights and some
Not bad, not good, more to follow

Tomorrow should never ever arrive
And today yesterday will be past
Because from today tomorrow will derive
Every day that could be your last.

Maddy Olley (12)
Ripon Grammar School, Ripon

My Dog!

I love my dog,
She likes to play,
I take her for a walk every day.
She loves to make friends
And enjoys her sleep,
She even likes playing hide-and-seek.
She wanders the garden,
Mostly in May,
She chases the rabbits every day.
She pulls a cute face,
Most of the time,
So then I can tell if she is mine!

Isobel Mitchell (11)
Ripon Grammar School, Ripon

Why War?

Why war?
Why do innocent people have to suffer for someone else's greed?
People don't deserve to die as a result of a bomb or a gunshot
Many live in poverty because of war
Why war?
Why not peace?
No bombs or guns
No demolished houses or treacherous sounds in the background
No fear of being shot when you're just leaving your own home
Just the silent sounds of the countryside or the blatant
                                        sounds of the city
It's not fair!
Why should some people live in a world of war and poverty
When others get a life of peace and luxury?
Should the world really be like this?

Katie Wade (11)
Ripon Grammar School, Ripon

The Eagle

The eagle glided above the trees
Twisting and turning like an acrobat
Watching the ground with his telescope of an eye
Watching, waiting
Patiently patrolling the forest
Waiting
Suddenly he saw it
The eagle dived down
Dodging branches
Crashing through the trees
Piercing the forest like a knife through butter
Skimming the ground before soaring back up
Its prize in its talons.

Jack Richards (12)
Ripon Grammar School, Ripon

Seasons

Spring is when
the frogspawn,
the baby lambs are born
and the seeds we sow, grow,
into corn to make our dough.

Summer is when
the bees hum,
the warm weather does come
and tourists travel to different places,
carrying their enormous cases.

Autumn is when
the clocks go back,
then the nights are really black,
leaves fall to the ground,
fireworks make a big loud sound.

Winter is when
snowflakes fall,
we roll them up to make a ball,
Christmas is here, hip hip hooray,
we'll wait for the next Christmas Day.

Jodie Simpson (12)
Ripon Grammar School, Ripon

Insect Life

I'd love to know what an insect's life is really all about
And when you see a big fat spider you definitely want it out,
You hear a buzzing fly hovering outside your door
And then you see a woodlouse dancing on the floor.
You go outside and accidentally step upon a bee,
Oh well, it was already dead (I hope it wasn't me).
I really do hate greenflies flitting near my tree
And I hope there aren't any insects squirming in my tea!

Louiza Whiteley (11)
Ripon Grammar School, Ripon

The Bully

He pushed me over
I scraped my knee,
The bully was laughing
And laughing with glee.

I went home crying
To my dad,
He looked at me
And felt so sad.

He couldn't help
Except one thing,
He went to school
As my king.

He told that bully
'I dare you.'
My dad said, 'No!
Good riddance to you.'

I went to school
All happy with glee,
This time he looked like
He'd scraped his knee.

Jonathan Walker (12)
Ripon Grammar School, Ripon

Christmas Time

Hooray, hooray, it's Christmas time!
Down your chimney St Nick will climb.
Presents are piled up around the tree,
Hopefully one will be addressed to me.

Hooray, hooray, it's Christmas time!
Christmas trees will shimmer and shine.
Snowflakes fall on my face and nose,
Exploding with light, the north star glows.

Guy Buckle (11)
Ripon Grammar School, Ripon

The Worst Bit Of School Dinners

Watery custard and mushy peas,
Won't somebody get some nice food please?
Good to bad and bad to good,
Some of it even tastes like mud!

Some are cooked and some are not,
Some are the colour of manky snot!
The salt is the sugar and the sugar is the salt,
Won't someone please put it to a halt?

The water is murky, the bread is stale,
Hopefully our attempt to stop it won't fail!
Squished tomatoes and runny sauce,
Soon we may have to use brutal force!

All of the pizza is brown to the crust,
Please get some cooks that we can trust!
Rotten eggs and smelly fish
Aren't exactly our choice of dish!

Cold hot dogs without a bun,
Really aren't a lot of fun!
If we don't get it sorted out soon,
We might have all met our doom!

Yasmin Rogers (12)
Ripon Grammar School, Ripon

Bands

The pain of my arm while I am in the mosh pit
The screech of the girls while I am playing my guitar
The beat of the drum while getting kicked up the bum
The boom of the bass
The scream of the stage divers
The bang of the gun - that *vicious* shot

They are the things that makes a real band.

Christian Hair (11)
Ripon Grammar School, Ripon

Fashion Passion!

Saturday morning in the busy town,
Lots of people running up and down.
Walking towards the shops and stores,
In I go through the electric doors.
There I was looking left and right,
Seeing what clothes there were in sight.
Shopping, shopping, it's my passion,
How I love the latest fashion.

I stepped inside a big chain store,
That I had not been in before.
All I could see was lots of trousers,
T-shirts, skirts, jackets and blouses.
Looking through the rails of all these things,
Some of them suitable for queens and kings.
Shopping, shopping it's my passion,
How I love the latest fashion.

But there it was the coat of my dreams,
With bright pink stitches down all the seams.
Then I realised how much it would cost
And all at once my dreams were lost.
All of a sudden I let out a wail,
When I saw the coat was in the *sale!*
Shopping, shopping, it's my passion,
How I love the latest fashion.

Eloise Robinson (12)
Ripon Grammar School, Ripon

My Family

My sister is a chatterbox,
She never shuts up,
Chatter, chatter, chatter,
Is all we ever hear,
She often shouts and blabbers,
She will always be making noise,
Whether or not it makes sense,
Is a totally different matter.

My mother is so kind,
She always cooks and cleans,
She does all of my washing
And often buys me sweets.

My brother is so boring,
He never plays with me,
He's always on his games console,
Sat upstairs inside his room.

My father is in charge,
He is the sergeant of the house,
He works for the police
And can sort anybody out!

And then there is me,
I'm *perfect!*

Rachel Osborne (11)
Ripon Grammar School, Ripon

Fashion

All the new gear
Is all the rage in fashion.
So if you wear these labels
You'll look great with style and passion

So these amazing labels
Bench and Goldigga
Are designer and expensive
And will spice up your figure

Wear these fantastic items
Quicksilver and O'Neill
Gorgeous, fantastic, great
That's what they'll make you feel

Here is some advice
To look funky and look cool
Wear these amazing accessories
So you don't look like a fool.

Freya Mortimer (11)
Ripon Grammar School, Ripon

Nissan Skyline

N issan Skyline out on the motorway,
I ts exhaust fumes pumping into the air.
S ilver sparkling in the sun.
S izzling the road at max speed,
A police car, nowhere, to catch the dart.
N ibbling fingers the other drivers swear.

S pilling drinks as the beast flies by,
K icking in, the engine revs,
Y aris Toyota is no match.
L and Rovers have no chance.
I s there a car faster than this?
N issans rule
E very day!

Jonathan Coates (11)
Ripon Grammar School, Ripon

Sailor And Me

That sailor yonder went to sea,
He sailed down the Norfolk Broads with me.
He taught me what was port and starboard,
Now I know what is wood and cardboard.

Whilst spinning yarns and eating meat,
I learned of mermaids and sea serpents neat,
Of ale so strong it made you sleep,
Oh those such stories they made me weep.

Our ship, The Crosswire, fine was she,
As she sailed in the deep blue sea,
Carved an angel on her bow
And on her helm was half a cow.

Spent many an hour in the crow's nest,
Whilst old cook would knit a vest.
Then sailor shouted to come down,
For he preferred it on the ground.

Plenty of treasure we did find,
But the pirates were not very kind.
Then foreign land we did hit,
Old sailor stayed, the silly twit.

Jessica Priestley (13)
Ripon Grammar School, Ripon

Snowflakes

A snowflake is like a person,
No two are the same,
Each different in some way.

Falling to the ground,
To join the others.

Lasting but a little while,
Just to fade away.

To then be reborn.

Rachel Cunningham (14)
Ripon Grammar School, Ripon

Little Girl

Little girl crying in the rain,
Lots of tears and lots of pain.
Little girl don't know what to do,
In her place, you wouldn't too.

Little girl knows it didn't go right,
Cries and cries throughout the night.
Little girl knows just what is true,
More than me, more than you.

Little girl spat on in the yard,
Growing up is very hard,
Little girl don't know who to tell,
Every day another hell.

Little girl sits down to cry,
Sometimes wishes she could die.
Little girl needs you today,
Don't pass her by, don't turn away.

Nicole Hutton (13)
Ripon Grammar School, Ripon

The Wild Horse

Roaming and eating on the moor,
Black as the night or a beautiful bay,
Jumping and trotting through a river,
Splashing and drinking in the day.

Rolling like a ballerina in the sand,
Climbing up a rocky hill,
Racing other foals in play,
Sheltering in an old mill.

When a horse is free,
Looking across a lake of glass,
Seeing its reflection,
Galloping wildly over a blanket of grass.

Kiera Chapman (12)
Ripon Grammar School, Ripon

A Cat's View To Human Beings

Miaow miaow
humans don't
understand always yelling
at me not to bring in presents
waking me up when I have just
found a comfortable, warm, woolly
thing to sit on - it's their best
'jumper'

So what!
No eating the Christmas turkey
no mice
no birds
no muddy paws
no scratching
no comfortable napping places
what am I supposed to do?

Jessica Burgess (11)
Ripon Grammar School, Ripon

Autumn

The golden leaves fall from the trees,
The wind whistles in your ear.

The rain taps against the window,
Waiting to be let in.

Conkers drop on your head,
As you shelter from the rain.

Flowers are dull and lonely,
Hail lashes against their petals,
Killing them off one by one.

As snow begins to form,
Winter starts to dawn.

Rosie Tattersall (12)
Ripon Grammar School, Ripon

Forgotten

Ancient, long forgotten and dejected
That is you,
O' Pagan gods of old

Great shrines built in your honour
Now old, derelict and unremembered
O' Pagan gods of old

Civilisations built on your existence
Races brought together on hearing your names
O' Pagan gods of old

Every continent, country, county
Had their own, but all were you
O' Pagan gods of old

Victories won for you, all the honour yours
Legions worshipped and adored you
O' Pagan gods of old

Your lives contained within the pages of a book
Ages have been past and still you remain
O' Pagan gods of old

Sacrifices, dreams and lives were yours
But you have been forgotten
O' Pagan gods of old.

Clare Burnett (13)
Ripon Grammar School, Ripon

Waterfall

Water falls off the edge into the unknown
Fish try and try but will never get up
Smashing into the rocks sending waves along the surface
The rays glisten off the falling rush of water in the morning sunshine
A wonderful sight and a wonder of the world.

Alec Graham (11)
Ripon Grammar School, Ripon

Fireworks

I
Like
Fireworks
The way they fly
Scream
Screech
Crackle
Then die!
The boom
The cry as
They reach
For the sky
Explosions!
And colours
Red, green, blue
B
A
N
G
!

Jack Park (12)
Ripon Grammar School, Ripon

I Wish . . .

Can't change the world but if I could,
I'd make you have me and me have you.
I wish the light would never fade,
That my choices had already been made,
I wish that it didn't take forever and a day,
To tell someone you love them in your own way,
I wish our love was out in the open,
For if no one knows love isn't true,
Someone special told me this but I don't agree,
Cos I know what I'm feeling when I'm with you.

Natalia de Hutiray (12)
Ripon Grammar School, Ripon

Home Is . . .

Home is a place of safety yet imprisonment
Home is suffocating when you're not free to leave
Home is a jail when you're unhappily grounded
Home is . . .

Home is somewhere cold in winter
Home is a crumbling building falling down around you
Home is a small house standing in a huge garden
Home is . . .

Home is a place with or without parents
Home is a place with or without animals
Home is a place with or without everything you want
Home is . . .

Home is a place you take for granted
Home is a place you have to leave
Home is always around for you
Home is . . .

Hannah Olsen Shaw (11)
Ripon Grammar School, Ripon

The Sparkle Of A Blue Topaz

I look into those eyes and they look back
They glisten in the light
I love that pretty sight
The bright blue envelopes me
Like rolling in a sea
They rid me of fears
And take away my tears
My feelings come ablaze
When I meet your beautiful gaze
I look into those eyes and they look back
And that is why they sparkle like a blue topaz.

Adam Lister (15)
Ripon Grammar School, Ripon

Tired

I'm tired of being angry,
I'm tired of being jealous.
I'm tired of screaming,
I'm tired of crying.
I'm tired of hurting people,
I'm tired of being hurt.
I'm tired of loving,
I'm tired of not being loved.
I'm tired of listening,
I'm tired of not being heard.
I'm tired of trying,
I'm tired of failing.
I'm tired of me,
I'm tired of you.
I'm tired of this,
I'm tired of life.

Leanne Hanrahan (15)
Ripon Grammar School, Ripon

Cats

They lie; curled up enjoying the warmth of the bright hot flames,
They rest; embedded in fresh towels or quilt covers peacefully
                                    drifting off into endless sleep,
They lap; creamy, warm milk with their small rough tongue,
They munch; crunchy meat biscuits until their heart's desire,
They wash; spending hours cleaning their colourful, soft, silky
                fur until not a single speck of dust can be seen,
They prowl; their surroundings inspecting every object, every
            corner, every cobweb, as if protecting their home from danger,
They pounce; outside in search of small birds, mice, moles
And other creatures, their instinct is to kill, living the life of a
                                    predator, finding food to eat.

For cats' wildness still lies inside of them, their sense of purpose is to
protect and look after only themselves at all times, for nobody can be
trusted.

Frances Shaw (12)
Ripon Grammar School, Ripon

Diana

Rising above the seas,
Sinking below the hills.
You are the one who stares
At the sun, right into his eyes.
Control of the night, its creatures
Totally at your will
Misuse them is not what you do.
Watch the unicorns dance, the dragons fly,
Running with brumbies, racing rivers
Free to dance in the hills
With the unseen spirits
Nothing to worry for
But walk hand in hand
With loneliness
No one to sacrifice a white bull for
Or morn the loss of your kingdom.
But look for me, day or night.
I will be there, watching, waiting
When the clouds serve not as our enemy
And the stars are our messengers.
I will wait for your ghostly presence
Reflecting the light of my eyes
And I will mourn your loss,
And I will hold your hand.
All I ask for
Is your friendship and guidance
To face the cruel son of evil tomorrow
And navigate through the maze of iniquity
The qualities of true friends we will share.

Lauren Fielding (15)
Ripon Grammar School, Ripon

Alone

She walks alone with her head face down,
Trying to attract as little attention as possible.
In every step she makes no sound,
She has no friends at all.

Every joke is aimed at her,
Her eyes swell up in tears,
Though no one around her can see her pain,
She's felt this way for years.

Going back home from school, should seem a relief,
But for her it's another nightmare,
For still at home she suffers abuse
And gets no love or care

She enters the kitchen late at night
And takes a knife from the drawer
She slits the knife hard across her left wrist
And out the blood does pour

Deep red blood, the colour so sweet
She starts to feel so faint
She tries to stagger upstairs to her room
But she trips and it's too late

Her head slams back against the wall
In the back of her head her eyes roll around
Her breathing grows heavy, she starts to shake
And in no time at all she makes no sound.

Emily Davies (14)
Ripon Grammar School, Ripon

Mirror Image

I love the way you look at me,
I hate it when you don't call,
I love the way you love me,
I hate how I feel so small.
I love the way you want me,
But only for a while,
I love it you'd do anything for me,
I hate the way you smile.
I love the way you kiss me,
I hate the way you lie.
I love it when you're happy,
But it's worse to see you cry,
I love the way you hold me,
I hate it when you take your time,
I love the way you touch me,
I hate it when you take what's mine,
I love the way you praise me,
I hate it when I wait for you,
I love it when you call me,
If you haven't noticed, I love/hate too.

Jess Warren (14)
Ripon Grammar School, Ripon

War

There was a blazing ball of fire flying through the cold, wet,
murky sky and that was when I knew the war had begun.
They ran from the right, they ran from the left; there was death
coming from all parts of the battle.
Finally the war had ended, there was one man left, and he didn't
know why it had begun.

Dave Marsden (14)
Ripon Grammar School, Ripon

Springtime

Flowers burst open, a beautiful sight to see,
Giving off a pleasant scent for every single bee,
Growing taller every day,
The petals bloom in every way.

Farmers get up early every morning,
For lambs are being born without a warning,
Before you know it they'll be up on their feet,
Waiting for other lambs to meet.

Around the fields rabbits hop,
Never having time to stop,
Bunnies waggle their fluffy white tails,
When jumping over the garden rails.

So much happening in the season of spring,
It's a time for the birds to come out and sing,
Let's enjoy it while it lasts,
As this season goes so fast.

Charlotte Frank (12)
Ripon Grammar School, Ripon

My Visit To London

London, the capital,
London, the heart of England.
Museums to visit, sights to see,
Important buildings and places to be.
The latest thing to see is the eye,
It reaches up and up to the sky.
A ride on this is such a thrill,
The memory is in my mind still.
The palace, the tower, the Thames and all,
The parks, the square and the pigeons' call.
London, the heart,
London, the capital of England.

Carrie Turner-Fryatt (12)
Ripon Grammar School, Ripon

News Of The World

Have you read the paper lately
About all the hate and conflict
What's going wrong with the world?
Why all the crimes and hurting?

Two wrongs don't make a right
But tell Bush and Blair that
They seem to think because of a few evil people
That thousands of innocents should suffer

People are getting greedy and obese
Do you ever think about those who starve?
People suffer and die every day
But do you even care or are you just selfish?

And why would you give a girl of fourteen
Her miscarried foetus to take home
And put in the fridge as though it's a snack?
Has she not been through enough?

All these celebrities say that they are
But how many actually do something to help?
They are so bothered about their image
That they'll say anything to look good

There are so many cold-hearted killers
Do they even stop and think
About all the people that'll be affected
Or what they'd do if they were in the opposite position?

What about all the binge drinkers
Are you not aware of the risks?
But what is even dumber is if you get in a car
And drive because your reactions are slower when drunk

Who would want to give birth to a baby
And let it grow up in a world like this?

Alison Fraser (15)
Ripon Grammar School, Ripon

Thoughts On Space

Space: the final frontier -
Why?
Is there anything further than space
That we should explore?
How would we get there?
A rocket,
A spacecraft,
A shuttle,
A meteor -
What an adventure that would be!
Time
Is affected by space travel:
What time would it be when we got there?
Could we arrive before we set off?
Would Earth even be there?
A black hole -
Tunnel vision?
Wouldn't a light hole be better?
Would we meet anyone on the way?
Explorers from other planets
Looking for the same answers.
Could we help each other?
Maybe they already have the answer.
Should we ask them or find out for ourselves?
Satisfaction is
Learning for ourselves,
Making our own mistakes
And learning from them.
Is that the better path to choose?
What do you think?

James Clarke (13)
Ripon Grammar School, Ripon

My Unintended Choice

I'm thinking about you
I'm afraid
You make me feel things I don't understand
I can't lose you
You mean so much to me
You could mean even more
If I could tell you
The way I see you
Not just a friend
But so much more besides
I have no words
We're so close
But so far apart
And if I'm wrong
I could drive you away
I know you care
But I don't know how much
And the thought of you
Makes my heart ache
And I wait
For the next time I see you
I should probably say something
But I can't find the right way
So I sit
And think about you.

Maggie Ellis (15)
Ripon Grammar School, Ripon

Poison

Like sweet, addictive poison
You are life to me.
I am weak and vulnerable with you
But without you I'm dead.
I curl up in a ball so small
You suffocate me.
Smother me with your selfish, greedy love
Impounding obsession fractures my delicate bones.
Your touch is ecstasy
But blindingly painful.
You breathe life into me with your kiss.
A prisoner to your love.
You warm me,
I crumble.
I breathe through you,
We are one.
I am lost,
You consume me.
Too weak to move,
Or runaway
From you.
I need you.
But hate you.
Despise you.
Love you the most I could.

Emily Cottrell (15)
Ripon Grammar School, Ripon

Daddy's Girl

A girl needs her daddy
For many things like calling
Her dolly and pushing her
On swings

Decided not to tell you I was
Getting my belly done
You weren't too cross, you just said
'Umm, looks cool hun'

I will need picking up
Late Dad, I know this
Skirt looks quite short
But it's not too bad

On my way out, you give me
One of those looks, I ask
What you're thinking, you say
'Look at my baby, all grown up'

I'm sorry for all the times
I have acted ungrateful
I know it's not smart
But I hope you will always know
I'm a daddy's girl at heart.

Amber Gilliam (15)
Ripon Grammar School, Ripon

The Eternal Battle

Doomed ones dance with blades like thunder
Swords burrow deep in foes' chests
Cannons exhale and grind with iron spit
Lucifer hungrily waits for more minions of death

Warriors surge like raging rivers
They battle when the dragon consumes the sky
Deafening screams ring through your ears
And pierce the dark corners of your mind

A father dies to save his son
A lone unit charges and waits for death's sweet embrace
A siren shouts and hunts for the damned
The day succumbs to the ever hungry night

Years pass and the warriors long dead
Wait in the mountain to rise again
The battle rages on for a time eternal

Fire, water, day and night
Malevolent sincere death and life

The eternal battle of good and evil
Which like the phoenix never dies
The eternal battle of death and life.

Luke Haggerty (12)
Ripon Grammar School, Ripon

Skin Deep

I read of all your trophies
And all the wealth you reap,
I see a thing of beauty,
But is it just skin deep?

I see you in the movies
And glossy magazines,
Posing on the catwalk,
In that glamour fashion scene.

Tear away the façade
And throw it in the bin,
Then may we get a glimpse
Of what really lies within.

Yes you may be famous
And all the world's your stage,
You captivate your audience
With what you do being all the rage.

Look into the mirror,
Wipe away the veil,
Take away that image
And show us what is real.

I read of all your trophies
And all the wealth you reap,
I see a thing of beauty,
But is it just skin deep?

Jamie Horn (15)
Ripon Grammar School, Ripon

Beautiful Mind

You came for me, I did not fight,
You brought me to a world of white, not pure, but white,
There is evil in this place,
You say it's written in my face,
You think I cannot understand,
But I assure you that I can, I can,
I'm like the bone collector,
Only I collect those spiteful words,
Those you think I haven't heard,
I know every prime number up to 7507,
That's not you but me,
What is the world, who am I?
And why am I destined to die?
All these questions and all these lies,
As common as the blue in the skies,
You call me crazy, but not to my face,
You say we're all weird in this antiseptic place.
You chain me up when I get scared,
I kick and struggle, life's not fair,
White is meant to look clean,
But the bacterium, everywhere, everywhere,
They're in my clothes, in my hair.
You call it Asperger's Syndrome,
Some just say I'm a psychopath,
They call it emotionally distorted,
My mother called it my beautiful mind, until I killed her.

Sophie McEvoy (14)
Ripon Grammar School, Ripon

Life

Does anybody actually know what life means
Or can anyone define life?
Everyone has one, everyone lives one but what is one?
Is it the fact that we are living and breathing?
Or is it the things we do, the people we know or the people we are?
Each human being can make a life and everyone can save lives,
So does that mean that life is the fact that we are alive and breathing,
From the moment we are born till the moment we die, we are living life,
We go to school, get jobs, get married, have children and then die, so
Is that it, is that life?
Maybe life is the emotions we feel, the people we love in all sorts of
Ways and just the simple fact that we are here,
Or life could be indefinable; maybe it has a different
Meaning for everyone
And maybe it is one of those things that us humans will never
Understand or truly appreciate.

Katie Fortune (14)
Ripon Grammar School, Ripon

Soldier Boy

I wish I could be a soldier like my dad,
My gun at my side, only me and my pride,
I would fight to the very last.
I would arrive home, my gun still at my side, everyone cheering me on,
Oh, the glory of fighting for my country,
How I practised with toy gun and waited for my time to come.

Now that I am here, I see beyond my boyish dreams,
Now I see the blood, the sweat, the tears.
The guns battle on, the barrage unceasing,
The wounded lay in agony alone wailing for help,
Soldiers made mad by their terror sobbing,
Cowering in my trench with my gun still by my side . . .

How wrong could I be?

Joseph Priestley (12)
Ripon Grammar School, Ripon

Worthiness

The man who was,
Was young and slick,
The man who came,
Was old and frail.

The man who was,
Was fit and strong,
The man who begged,
Was weak and feeble.

The man who was,
Was happy and lively,
The man who cried,
Was sad and tired.

The man who was,
Was proud and outgoing,
The man who was cast aside,
Was ashamed and shy.

The man who was,
Was a liar and a cheat,
The man who knew,
Was honest and true.

Edward Lilley (14)
Ripon Grammar School, Ripon

The Clock

Hands whirling and whirling
Learning to count
The start of a day
The end of a year
Whirling . . .
Whirling . . .

Ben Wright (13)
Ripon Grammar School, Ripon

Here I Am

Here I am
Standing all alone
No friends, no games, no fun
There he is
Striding along
Come to torment me in my loneliness

Isn't it enough
That no one likes me
Isn't it enough
That he caused this pain
Obviously not

I turn now, for run I must
Or pain beyond all belief follows
Run I shall, into the building
Where maybe I can hide for a while
Here he comes, following me
I twist, I turn but no path is laid before me

The stairs! The stairs! Up, up, up
Now the top I reach and turning see
A wonder of enormity
Oh! Fallen is he

Down I climb and as I come, he lifts his face in fear
But even as my mind prepares, to torment as did he
My heart cries, give aid, give aid and help
So stretching out my hand I help and take it does he
And now as our eyes meet he speaks his thanks
And goes on a better way.

Theo Parker (11)
Ripon Grammar School, Ripon

Down At The Bottom

The current was strong
And it pulled me down.
Down to the bottom
Where there was no sound.

There I could think,
Be alone for a while.
Of his fervent grip
And his forlorn smile.

His face in my mind,
Full of wanting,
Maybe for me to live,
Did I want to?
Either way I could not forgive.

He need not speak,
Actions were enough.
To show what he wanted,
He need not bluff.

He's driven me here,
Down to the bottom,
Here I lay,
On the verge of forgiving,
But it's too late,
It's here I'll stay . . .

Down at the bottom.

Megan Wright (13)
Ripon Grammar School, Ripon

The Match

The two teams came out
The fans began to shout
What will the match bring?

A goal is scored
No one's bored
What a very good thing

The forward missed
A man used his fist
This is only one match

The goalie coughed
The player got sent off
That was the end of him!

The whistle's gone
The fans had fun
And no one lost a limb!

Liam Evans (11)
Ripon Grammar School, Ripon

World War

Machine guns blazing
Armoured tanks rolling
Silent bombers in black, black skies

Deep, muddy trenches
Blood-red wounds
Cries and screams, shouts from nowhere

Then an eerie quiet
Calm, but not peaceful
Ceasefire. A result.

Total destruction
Deep, dark death.

Charlie Stelling (12)
Ripon Grammar School, Ripon

Untitled

I'm quiet as death as I enter the lagoon,
I reach to my side, pick up the harpoon,
I stare into the water's grey,
Where all is dark, never day . . .

All at once the water starts to boil,
I can feel my blood turn and toil,
Then all the ripples start to smooth out,
I'm about to see what the fuss is about . . .

Then a turquoise tail shimmers down below,
I check all around me, desperate to go,
But I cannot leave 'til my task is complete,
Even if it means that *she* and I meet.

Then the ripples turn to waves and I hear a scream,
That means that *she* must be in a mood supreme.
No one can do it if I die,
I bet I can't kill *her*, but at least I can try.

There *she* is, sliding through the water!
There are two more beside her, must be *her* daughters,
I'm destined to die, it's three against one,
I'm smothered by darkness, now the sun has gone.

My screams are heard all over the lagoon,
While *her* teeth sink into me, I start to throw my harpoon,
Then my outstretched arm is caught in a snare,
It's *her* daughter's teeth, hidden by her hair.

Two wandering men, found me when dead,
There were two deep teeth marks in my head,
Said, one, 'He tried to kill *her*, but all in vain,
For the mermaid of misery, wins again.'

The moral is:
If you think you are beaten, you are.

Isobel Jennings (11)
Ripon Grammar School, Ripon

Unknown

Walking, walking,
Walking into the unknown;
Can't stop, won't stop,
Walking, walking,
Walking into the unknown.

Looking, looking,
Looking for the lost;
Can't stop, won't stop,
Looking, looking,
Walking into the unknown.

Feeling, feeling,
Feeling for what I want to know;
Can't stop, won't stop,
Feeling, feeling,
Walking into the unknown.

Tasting, tasting,
Tasting what I have come to hate;
Can't stop, won't stop,
Tasting, tasting,
Walking into the unknown.

Listening, listening,
Listening for how to ease my pain;
Can't stop, won't stop,
Listening, listening,
Walking into the unknown.

Edward Riley (12)
Ripon Grammar School, Ripon

The Greedy fox

'Twas on a hot summer's afternoon,
The sun shone bright,
All was still.
Then the fox came out of his hole,
For he had a plan to kill,
Some little plump chickens.
He strolled down the fields,
Towards the farm of Ted's,
He sharpened his claws.
He saw them,
His victims,
Just waking up.
He crept up behind
And *snap*,
He had one in his mouth.
It wasn't long until he ate all of them,
Every single one,
Poor little things.
Then the farmer woke up,
Heard the fox
And grabbed his gun.
Silence, silence
And then *bang*,
The fox fell dead.

So let that be a lesson to the lot of you.
You shouldn't take more than you need.
Never.

Greg Munsch (12)
Ripon Grammar School, Ripon

I Don't Know What To Write A Poem About!

My teacher gave our form some homework
On Monday she said, '1C
Your homework is to write a poem
And hand it back to me'
I didn't tell my mum the truth and rushed straight out to play
So tonight I'm sitting here puzzled completely in dismay
Because . . .
I *don't* know what to write a poem about

I went to my mum with the homework
And asked for some advice
But she said to get on with it
Which wasn't very nice
I came back to my room and sat there for ages and ages
Looking through books of poetry I must have read one hundred pages
But . . .
I *still* don't know what to write a poem about

My mum was getting crosser
As it was time to sleep
She said I shouldn't make her angry
Or she would make me weep
I walked into my room and then I finally got it
I'd put all my thoughts down on paper in case I forgot it
As . . .
I *now* know what to write a poem about

I've made a New Year's resolution
Although it's a bit too early
I think I've found the solution
For Mum to treat me fairly
When I get my homework I'll do it on the night
Because then I'll give myself a chance to try and get it right!

Thomas King (11)
Ripon Grammar School, Ripon

The Story Of Hallowe'en Night

Hallowe'en is a spooky night,
All the costumes gives me a fright,
Little devils, vampires, bats,
Witches, ghosts, monsters, rats,
Trick or treating is great fun,
Sweets and chocolates, cakes and buns,
As night falls the owl hoots,
Then I hear the clomping of boots,
As I turn around to see,
A howling vampire staring at me.

I run and run with all my might,
Trembling with a terrible fright,
At last I reach home, sweet home,
I seem to lose the evil moan,
I knock once upon the door,
And in a few seconds, maybe more,
Roaring, raging monster bold,
He opens the door, the breeze is cold,
I suddenly scream and drop my bun,
But then I realise it's only my mum!

Curling up by the fire,
Heavy eyelids as I tire,
Looking deep into the flames,
My mind again is playing games,
Round the cauldron witches dance,
Luring me into a trance,
Nightmare, building in my head,
Now they're burning little Ted,
'Bedtime,' shouts Auntie Mable,
Wide awake, dreams disable.

Jessica Lyall (11)
Ripon Grammar School, Ripon

Schooldays

When I was four
I could colour all day
And then colour some more,
But then the teacher would say,
'Children, it's home time.'

When I was seven,
I took my first SATs,
I was hardly in Heaven,
But I knew that
It would be home time soon.

When I was nine,
I worked really hard,
My school life was fine,
Then I would pack up my books
And once again it was home time.

When I was eleven,
I said my final goodbye,
To teacher, Mr Evan,
Many tears were shed,
Before the last home time.

Now I'm thirteen,
I have eight lessons a day,
I try to keep up and stay keen,
But really I can't wait,
For the bell to ring, *home time.*

Polly Sands (13)
Ripon Grammar School, Ripon

Love Hurts In Many Ways

Hot tears of anger roll down my bruised face
You look deep into my watering eyes
I lie there against the cold stone walls sobbing
Why do you do this to me?
You reach out, I push you away
You say you love me
But that doesn't make up for it
But still I carry on doing everything for you

A new day, a fresh start
I know you don't mean to hurt me
But I forgive you
You go out, you don't return
What has happened?
I hear the creak of the door
I rush down the stairs
Those were my last steps
I approach you and . . .

An agonising seer of pain shoots up my chest
I can't breathe, you slowly fade away
But now I'm OK
There's no pain, not anymore
And now I can see you clearly
I see you sitting on the floor, your head in your hands
Why are you ignoring me?
I look further across and see a lifeless, still body
I'm looking at . . . me.

Helen Anderson (11)
Ripon Grammar School, Ripon

Black Boy's Wish

My wish crept up my body from my feet
Until it reached my heart
And burned right through my ever-taunting skin,
The skin that meant so much.
Then my wish rolled up this skin,
As a paintbrush would up a wall,
To reach that piercing trickle of water
That represented my world, everything.

The frosty spit singed my sun-caked skin
As it dribbled down my ochred nose like a snail trail.

While crouching uncertainly, I was engulfed by the circle
Of interlocking hearts and minds around me
So my senses were overpowered until I was lost
In a whirlwind of hatred that chattered the flesh
That held my existence together.

The radiational power and loathing of this immense body
Enveloping me beat down on the surrounding creatures
Like algae in the ocean of spectation I was aware of.

As the embracement and entrancement mounted
As a great volcano out of the tides,
I found no place else to go but within my soul
And as I cascaded into its murky and puzzletatious depths
I found the answer that bewildered so many
Of those who taunt me, I found love.

Then warmth broke the heavy atmosphere like a ray of sunshine
Through darkened branches and the kindness bubbled
Into every corner of the world until every face,
Previously jeering with hate, was enlightened
In a calm harmony of peoples, united, not in colour of skin
Or of family influence, but in peace, and love
And the wish that isn't really a wish anymore,
But perhaps, if we make it, reality.

Amelia Tearle (12)
Ripon Grammar School, Ripon

Our War

Hatred is what causes war,
But imagine if there was no hatred,
Would it be entirely different or the same?

Money is also what causes the wars,
People who have money hate the poor,
But people who have nothing hate the rich,
What would it be like if we had the same?

Jealousy is also what causes the wars,
The smarter people get praise and glory,
Whilst the less intelligent people are left with nothing to be proud of,
But what would it be like if people were equal in mental
                                                    and physical games?

Bullying is also what causes the wars,
But it's usually the bullies, who have the worst problems,
Bullies usually take their anger out on other people due to
                                                    their past actions,
What would it be like if there were no problems in the world?

But in the end of all the wars we have to fight in our everyday lives,
There are no winners or losers,
But there will always be hope around the corner.

Joe Turner (12)
Ripon Grammar School, Ripon

Rocket

R ocketing, twisting, ripping the air into shreds, crippling hurtling,
O rbiting, rippling, crippling and flipping,
C rashing, attempting and failing, falling,
K icking out of the atmosphere,
E ager to land and to see Earth again,
T oday a trip into the unexplored.

Joshua Hill (12)
Ripon Grammar School, Ripon

Solomon

How I used to look at you, smiling all the time
While you purred and rubbed against me
And your knowing face stared into mine
I thought you loved me like family

Your soft whiskers tickled my cheek
Your creamy fur, silken to the touch
Your sapphire-blue eyes seemed to seek
The love you desired so much

But since that day I said goodbye
I've lost a friend so dear
Your spirit soared up to the sky
Happy and free

Oh, how these days have come and gone
Without you, feline noble one
Yet my heart is empty
And will always be

Now a feline has replaced you
With no such charms you possessed
I still long for your happy face and warm touch
You were the absolute best.

Alicia Hunt (11)
Ripon Grammar School, Ripon

Poem

Bravely I stood,
Upon this barren place.
Where had it gone?
Vanished without a trace.
All there is, is plains,
Existence is no more.
All life wiped out,
Just because of war.

Brooke Farrar (14)
Ripon Grammar School, Ripon

The Vampire

Drooling, slavering,
I wake up in the night.
My lips are red,
My face is white.
I feel my teeth;
They turned into fangs.
I go to the cellar
Where my wife hangs.
I go to the graveyard
To see my relations,
Who have been there
For many generations.
I transform to a bat
And fly into the night,
To glide around
And give people a fright.
I go to my coffin,
The haunting does cease.
I lay in my 'bed' to
Rest in peace.

Rory Buckle (11)
Ripon Grammar School, Ripon

Being

Out of control and out of my hands;
Balloon here is floating, but where will it land?
The Earth to explore without compass to guide,
Inside secure, only air mystified.
All there is to be done; all there is to be seen,
Head full of wonder and heart full of dreams.
Question the unquestionable, world shrinking at my feet.
Answer the unanswerable, unknown ends will meet.

Bryony Tallack (18)
Ripon Grammar School, Ripon

RIP Sparky (2002-2004)

My goldfish, I won at the fair,
I gave it to my little bro because I didn't care.
I woke up one morning, Sparky must have bumped his head,
Cos when I looked into his tank I could see that he was dead!

We put him in an envelope, for that great fish pond in the sky,
My brother dug a tiny hole and had a little cry.
I thought that this was stupid and really rather dim,
Because when I went out next morning,
The neighbour's cat had eaten him!

He lived a long yet boring life,
He looked so lonely, should have got a wife.
Swam around his fish tank, fast and darty,
So RIP to my goldfish, Sparky.

The moral of my story, if you don't know what to do,
Don't have a funeral in the garden, have a service in the loo!

Lauren Fox (14)
Ripon Grammar School, Ripon

Widerspruch

You see me staring at you, but you're not really there,
I hear your silent scream at me, why do I have to stare?
The room in which your presence holds, has no supporting walls,
There is no ceiling, is no floor, the second presence calls.
I look into your blinded eyes, you see me start to slide,
Life is what your presence defies, revealed and yet we hide.

The street in which we start to walk, hides darkness with its light,
As if he can't quite stand the constant battle with the night.
I hold your hand open but close to my mind
And silence talks through what you've done.
To me, over again, away from me you can't run.
I continue to stare your way, I don't know if you're aware,
You see me staring at you, but you're not really there.

Amy Kelsall (16)
Ripon Grammar School, Ripon

Highwayman

The highwayman mounts his horse,
The stallion speeds to the target,
A horse-drawn carriage in the distance,
The driver sees him too late.

The highwayman draws his pistol,
The carriage stops, a thud is heard,
The driver falls to the ground,
The passengers are held at gunpoint.

The highwayman demands their treasures,
Of gold, silver and jewels,
They quiver and shiver with fright,
As he gallops off into the night.

He returns home with his treasures,
Full of joy and glee,
This time they didn't catch him,
So he can ride again past Gallows Hill.

Matthew Hellard (13)
Ripon Grammar School, Ripon

The War

Running across the field into the fray,
Women at home will be crying this day,
As men load their weapons,
Ready to charge,
More of our soldiers arrive on a barge,
As aircraft above drop down their deadly load,
All around tanks explode,
What is the point of fighting it out
When we don't even know what it is about?
What is the point of fighting more?
Why can't we just end this war?

Moral:
Don't fight when you don't know what you are fighting for.

Connor Culver (12)
Ripon Grammar School, Ripon

The Old Man

There's a greedy old man who does not share,
Who lives upon the hill up there,
This is what happened one night,
It made our whole village tremble with fright.

He sat still in his chair,
Watching his roaring fire flair,
Not moving at all just into the flames he does stare,
A knock on the door awakes him from his glare,
And he sighed into the cold, dark air,
He peeks his eerie nose round to see who's there
And stumbles towards the door without care,
He opens the door and looks at who is there,
Confronting him is a young girl with fair hair,
With a poof of smoke she turns to a big brown bear
And eats him up without a care.

The bear still walks the woods at night when it's eerie,
Eating up people who are selfish and greedy.

Danielle Foster (13)
Ripon Grammar School, Ripon

She Is . . .

She is surrounded by a hurricane of depression
She is as lonely as a forgotten dream
She is the living dead
She is . . .

She is starved until not realising that she is all alone
She is wounded to not caring, scarred to the bone
She is silenced to her grave and never speaks a word
She is . . .

She is not loved by anyone, no one wants to know
She is sleeping in the gutters with nowhere else to go
She is living her worst nightmare in a suffocating dream
She is . . .

Francesca Fowden (13)
Ripon Grammar School, Ripon

Soulful

Deep into the soul she swam
Soul
What did it mean?
An immaterial part
Actuating cause of individual life
Linking spirit and matter
Or . . . nothing?
A feeling maybe
An emotion
Never-ending force behind us, forging our destiny
The inner, most sacred part of each person
Lasts forever, never began, never to end

She saw the love
She saw the hate
And all in-between
Jealousy towards enemies
Fear towards superstitions
Anger towards the world
Sympathy towards victims
Pride for family

She explored everything the soul felt
And found
It was completely
Different
To hers

Everyone is eternal
Eternal in soul
We will all live forever
If we believe.

Niki Delf (14)
Ripon Grammar School, Ripon

A Trip To The Dentist

I was in the dentist's waiting room,
It was going to happen soon, soon, soon,
A filling, a tooth out, a root canal,
The dentist is definitely not my pal.

The steps I took on the way to the room,
The look on my face only showed gloom,
I disheartedly sat in the dentist's chair,
Looking around, 'What's that over there?'
The syringe that was awaiting my gum,
The needle came in and my tooth went numb.

The look on my face said it all,
I couldn't help it, I was gonna bawl!
My mouth was greeted by a pair of pliers,
They said it wouldn't hurt, *liars!*

The blood and tears pouring,
My gum had been left mourning,
Without that tooth, my mouth is nothing,
Blood was the only thing I was coughing.

A few months later . . .

Ha, ha dentist, my tooth is back,
So, what did you get out of that?

Scot Bowman (13)
Ripon Grammar School, Ripon

Iceberg

All this pollution,
I feel myself turning into liquid,
I swim with the ocean,
We are so powerful,
We need more space,
Together we devour continents,
Conquered.

Kirsty Hall (11)
Ripon Grammar School, Ripon

Untitled

'There are more stars in the sky,
Than grains of sand on every beach in the world, did you know?'

They come thundering in the clouds tonight,
Powerful, huge and fierce like the 12ft roaring surf at Bedruthen steps,
Rolling, vivid 'white stallions' emerge, as they turn and crash.
Tumbling amongst each other, they scatter out.
Now small and bubbly, like when the tide reaches shallower water
The clouds slide over each other
And disappear into the star flooded sky.
As does the froth that disappears into the sand,
When it reaches the edge of the bay.

'There are more stars in the sky,
Than grains of sand on every beach in the world, did you know?'

And as the waves hide the sand, on the beach,
Like a mirror image
The clouds hide the stars in the sky.

Olivia Taylor (16)
Ripon Grammar School, Ripon

The Doll

The doll, her shiny porcelain cheeks,
Her golden curls that cascaded down her waist.

The sparkling blue eyes that really blinked,
The red velvet dress with the silk ribbons.

Her miniature shoes, with the silver buckles,
The lacy white petticoat with every last detail.

She now sits in the corner,
Gathering dust, dirt and ugliness.

Losing her once appealing appearance,
Now a lost and forgotten toy.

Emily Wall (11)
Ripon Grammar School, Ripon

Misleading Smiles

As I walk along this street,
I see all the people smile,
But their faces give them away,
They've been pretending for a while.

Their smiles don't reach their eyes,
They show what they feel inside,
But now I've become one of them,
I can't stop now, though I've tried.

As I walk along this street,
These people say to me:
'Love will save us,'
But how can this be?
Just look at what love gave us,
A world full of killing
And blood spilling,
That won't ever change.

Only a hero can save us,
But I'm not gonna stand here and wait.
It'll be the same end for him,
His eyes will show nothing but hate.

Sally Barrett (13)
Ripon Grammar School, Ripon

Dinner Time

D inner is a beautiful sight,
I t's the best part of the day,
N ibbling and gnawing at the meal,
N utritional value low.
E very day I'm enjoying it.
R acing through my body.

T oday it may be chicken,
I s there a better time of day?
M y dinner's better than yours,
E very day of every year.

Thomas Boyle (11)
Ripon Grammar School, Ripon

Lots Of Food And TV

Sad but true the tale I'll tell you,
The misery deep for Derrick Drew.
Truant now for goodness sake,
He mumbled lamely of bellyache.
As his mother left the drive,
To occupy himself he did strive.
His gaze rested on the telly,
Just before a growl from the belly.
Chocolate, crisps and Coke too,
Eyes not leaving the screen for a moment or two.
Watching square-eyed, natter, natter,
All the while growing fatter.
Cakes and biscuits he devours,
As minutes drag by into hours.
Derrick blob, the fool of the school,
Through his own gluttony is no longer cool.
So couch potato just beware,
Or you too may fare,
Just the same as Derrick Drew.

Ashley Lowe (11)
Ripon Grammar School, Ripon

Snap!

There was a boy in the ocean,
Who met a great white shark,
'Would you like to play snap?' he said,
'Of course,' replied the shark.

The boy shuffled the cards,
He dealt them out to them
And started playing the game,
They played for hours then . . .

'Snap!' . . . said the shark
And the boy was gone!

Ben Marsden (11)
Ripon Grammar School, Ripon

Only In Her Dreams

As silence slowly claimed her,
With darkness at her side.
She walked into her memories,
With no hope for it had died.

Sitting in the corner,
On the stone-cold floor.
Rocking back and forward,
As tears began to pour.

Her eyes began to wander,
Towards the faded place.
Where flames would dance and quiver,
Upon her forgotten face.

Her smile had long been lifeless,
Twisted by fleeting time.
Without him her life and words,
No longer seemed to rhyme.

He would subsist to her,
Throughout the forlorn night.
Haunting her feral dreams,
Pending the pure daylight.

And when she wakes
And finds him gone.
She knows he's waiting for her,
Till she joins him once again, she knows it won't be long.

She craved to slip into a dream,
To again press their hands together,
To take her final bitter breath
And close her eyes forever.

Nicola Blair (13)
Ripon Grammar School, Ripon

The Hunt

I smelt them before I heard them . . .
I heard them before I saw them . . .
And when I saw them, I ran, ran, ran for my life.
The hounds are chasing me;
I can her them licking their merciless jaws that are dripping with saliva.
Ready to pounce,
Rip,
Tear.
I can smell their bloodthirsty breath, longing for blood.
It smells like the blood of my brothers, my sisters, my father,
                                                    my mother.

I will be next.
No! I will beat them.
I carry on running.
What!
No!
I don't believe it!
There's a hole where I could hide from them.
But I am way ahead of them!
No, I will not hide, I will show them that I can win.
I carry on running.
No, I was wrong.
I've run so far, I can't run any longer.
My feet are bleeding, my legs throbbing with pain.
They are here.
The first hound leaps, misses.
The second hound leaps, misses.
The third hound strikes, his jaws close.
The hunt has ended.

Eleanor Duffield (11)
Ripon Grammar School, Ripon

My Dog

One day my dog, Scruff,
Saw next-door's cat, Posy,
Preening in our apple tree,
Scruff let out a sudden bark,
Posy didn't even flinch.

Scruff climbed the tree,
Just to annoy Posy,
But Posy didn't turn a whisker,
As Scruff scrambled up the tree.

Suddenly, Scruff fell off,
Rolled over three times
And gave a sharp bark.

Scruff was furious with Posy,
Because his plan wasn't working!
So he quickly ran towards the tree
And jumped into its branches!

In surprise,
Posy tumbled out the tree,
As Scruff landed in the tree.
All I can say is,
At least cats have nine lives!

Anna-Marie Grundy (11)
Ripon Grammar School, Ripon

Warning, Brother's Room

Warning, warning, the reality is dawning,
My brother's room awaits in the morning.

Dare to enter the saturating pit,
Dare to go in. Edge bit by bit.
Dare to step inside, I already feel sick.

The smell from inside, the mess on the floor,
This is what I imagine and much, much more,
Not to go in should be a law.

But oh no it's not, I have to proceed,
The suspense and the dread, a warning they heed.

Here goes nothing, I'm all ears and eyes,
It could be a trap, a death pit in disguise,
But boy was I wrong, did I get a surprise.

The shelves neat and tidy, the bed neatly made,
No mess, no junk, we'd all just been played,
I was actually looking forward to visiting again.

Uh oh, he heard the bad part, now he's in a mood,
I should never have said that, never presumed.

To jump the gun was wrong of me,
I owe him now an apology.

Anna Feltham (11)
Ripon Grammar School, Ripon

Stars

Stars are sprinkled like salt, sparkling; sparkling.
They hold their own against the infinite vastness,
Paler, paler it turns as dawn approaches,
Tinges of pink and purple hinting, as blue starts
To take over.
Wispy feather-clouds streak the sky;
The golden sun peeps over the horizon,
Sending its rays to light up the world.
Clouds float to and fro all day,
Then the sun starts to hide its head and goes fire-orange,
Darker blues set in as the sunlight fades,
The lady moon shows
Her ghostly face,
Stars reappear shining, shining,
As the everlasting ebony-black takes over,
Once again.

Lillian Duffield (13)
Ripon Grammar School, Ripon

My View

As I am flying I see lots of things,
Trees, deserts, ponds, rivers, lakes,
But as I am flying, I don't see the real beauty of everything,
I just see the tops of trees,
The desert seems flat,
The ponds seem like puddles,
The rivers like streams
And the lakes are just ponds,
People think flying is great
And people think you see the beauty of the world,
You do, but when you're up here
You forget what things look like, from the side,
Or from below, so I would swap this place with anyone,
Just to learn what everything is
And what it looks like.

Adam Thompson (11)
Ripon Grammar School, Ripon

Friendship

Friendships come and friendships go,
Always there when you're feeling low,
There to share the good times
And to struggle through the bad,
You may share different interests,
But a friendship never rests,
There will be the arguments
And the times when you're not speaking,
They always have their bad patches,
But good friends don't come in batches,
You feel sad when split up,
But that's not necessarily bad,
Sharing secrets, clothes and lice,
Hugs, compliments, advice,
Friendships comes and friendships go.

Emily Harkleroad (13)
Ripon Grammar School, Ripon

After The War

After the war . . .
After the war there was great joy,
Everyone rejoicing that the pain was gone,
No more suffering and stories to be told
Of loved ones gone and widows made.

After the war there were weeping families,
Standing where once there had been their house,
Searching for possessions engulfed by the fires,
Silent streets are broken by the fire engines screeching past.

Some stores are left standing but stripped of their insides,
People enquiring about where to find food,
Some people begging for food and shelter,
But the people in the street just walk on by,
After the war . . .

Helen Holmes (13)
Ripon Grammar School, Ripon

Seasons

Winter
Snow falls
Children playing joyfully
Out comes the sun
Melting snow slushes on feet
It's over

Spring
Leaves sprouting
Green and new
The weather getting hotter
Time to buy new clothes
Getting hotter

Summer
It's hot
Ice creams are melting
Out comes the paddling pool
Starting to rain

Autumn
Leaves falling
Brown and dead
Rustling on the floor
The weather is still cold
It's getting colder.

Aimée Warden (12)
Ripon Grammar School, Ripon

Unnoticed

Who notices the unnoticed?
Like the way the grass is cut
Or the door that creaks shut;
The bird that cries thrice each night
Or the way it jumps, to take flight.

Who notices the unnoticed?
The fine print at the end of a book,
The tree that fell and shook
A pattern from a carpet
Or the call of a blue tit.

Who notices the unnoticed?
For to become not noticed
You have to first be noticed
So nothing is unnoticed!

If something truly was unnoticed,
Thus it never existed.
For, with no person to see it,
Notice it, smell it, feel it,
Then it leaves nothing behind;
It never existed,
It wasn't unnoticed,
But nor was it noticed.

Pedro Crosby (14)
Ripon Grammar School, Ripon

A Trip To The Seaside

I'm going for a trip to the seaside
I'll splash and play in the waves
I'll maybe enjoy a donkey ride
And explore the spooky caves

At last we're here hooray, hooray!
Step out the car and smell the sea
We're going to have a fantastic day
Including fish and chips for tea

Let's go and buy a delicious ice cream
So much to choose from, I can't decide
I think I'll have the strawberry dream
And fill myself up from side to side

Let's build a sandcastle tall and wide
And dig a moat around it
Will it survive the incoming tide
Or slowly collapse bit by bit?

Let's go for a swim in the sea
Gosh it's cold, maybe I'll just paddle
Strong and brave I should be
And over the waves I'll straddle

Tired and weary we now all are
So pack up all your things
Trudge our way back to the car
And see what tomorrow brings.

Letty Thomas (12)
Ripon Grammar School, Ripon

Spaghetti

Spaghetti is curly,
Spaghetti is straight,
Spaghetti is tasty,
Spaghetti is great!
It makes my tummy rumble when I smell the scrummy sauce,
It makes my daddy grumble 'cause he doesn't like this course.
I like to wind it in a ball and slurp it down my throat,
It makes my mummy cross at me because it looks so gross.
Spaghetti is curly,
Spaghetti is straight,
Spaghetti is tasty,
Spaghetti is great!
I don't like it with salt and pepper,
I don't like it with peas,
I like it with Bolognese
And Parmesan cheese.
Spaghetti is amazing,
Spaghetti is so fun,
At the end of it all
Spaghetti is yum!
Spaghetti is curly,
Spaghetti is straight,
Spaghetti is tasty,
Spaghetti is great!

Moral:
The moral to this story as you can plainly see
If you don't like spaghetti, you don't like me!

Hannah East (11)
Ripon Grammar School, Ripon

Amber Eyes

White-gold disc, a silver moon
Amber eyes in darkened gloom
Silent wings above them fly
Silent tears of pain to cry
Skin to fur in fluid morph
Agonised cries are echoed forth
Mouth to muzzle, hand to paw
Battered form on leafy floor
Cracking bone and stretching limb
Human falls and beast will win
Pain recedes and bright stars shine
Creature stands, emits a whine
Sniffs the air and glances round
Paws on ground begin to pound
Fleeting arrow through the night
Amber eyes is out of sight
Lonely howl in fleeting rain
Waiting to be man again.

Heather Thornton (15)
Ripon Grammar School, Ripon

Muddled Over You

I fell awake at seven past thirty
And had a slice of toast cos I was thirsty,
The weatherman said it would be sunny,
So I bought a pair of wellies with no money,
I ran to the bus stop but the train had already gone,
A woman said there would be more but none,
So I ran into town on a bike
And bumped into some friends I don't like,
I found some money by a sleeper
And he said, 'Finders weepers, losers keepers.'
I said hello when I saw you at the mall
And now I don't feel muddled at all.

Stephanie Crookston (13)
Ripon Grammar School, Ripon

A Poem With No Name

Trapped, alone, dying inside, nowhere to turn, it's too hard to take
It's all my fault, I'm to blame, my body, a shell it's all so fake
I hate myself, the world I despise
Hate and pain I see through my eyes
I hate everything, him and everyone
Thinking about all the things he's done
I just don't think I can cope it's too much
Remembering each and every lingering yet forbidden touch
I've caused so much suffering, I need a way out
To hurt, to feel, to scream, to shout
I need to cry, to feel loved, maybe pain
I'll go crazy, mad, I need to explain
I feel so isolated but there's nobody around
I'm trying to cry out but I'm making no sound
I've been outcast; people watch, stop and stare
There's no one who understands, none of them care
I'm trapped alone, dying inside,
I've nowhere to turn, it's too hard to take
It's all my fault, I'm to blame, my body a shell, it's all so fake.

Roxanne Stewart (16)
Ripon Grammar School, Ripon

Pink Is . . .

Pink is . . .
Pink is the colour of the best electric guitars
Pink is the colour of punk rock hair
Pink is the best in the world
Pink is the colour of my bedroom
Pink is the colour surrounding me when I sleep
Pink is my etnies shoes
Pink is the colour of my favourite deck
Pink is the sound of a perfect riff
Pink is safe
Pink is warm!

Mathew Carle (11)
Ripon Grammar School, Ripon

Seasons

Spring rain in this time of year
But I do not hope to fear
As the trees are in full bloom
And warmth is coming soon

Oh good, summer's here at last
All the cold of winter's past
Children play out in the sun
And enjoy it's endless fun

Autumn now with colours bright
Bonfires glow in the moonlit night
Up in the air some fireworks fly
Another season passes by

The snow is like a cosy bed
But if you were in it, you'd be dead
The trees are now extremely bare
But please, please don't despair

All four seasons have gone past
And look, spring's here at last.

Hannah Darnbrough (13)
Ripon Grammar School, Ripon

My Brother

My brother is the colour pink
but a back-stabbing purple,
chicken nuggets on a plate
and tomato sauce all over the table.

He is a raining summer's afternoon
and a speeding MacLaren F1,
four pints of going-flat Coke
or a lynx chewing on your heel.

The comfort is by far the worst,
lying in bed without a cover but
too tired to move even a little.

Cameron Aitken (11)
Ripon Grammar School, Ripon

Hallowe'en Night

Silent and dark but for the moon,
The witches will be out very soon.
It's the night of Hallowe'en
And if you look carefully all sorts can be seen.
There's vampires, ghosts, cats and witches,
Out on this night to gather some riches.
The witches with warts as ugly as can be,
The vampires and ghosts running around free,
The pumpkins so pretty are bright like the stars,
I'm sure that aliens can see us from Mars.
We're out trick or treating,
All our friends we are meeting,
But we don't know who they are!
They could be from a land afar,
Round the corner comes a mummy,
I thought he looked pretty funny.
We had a great night, it was ever so spooky,
We got lots of goodies and plenty of money.

Emma Foster (13)
Ripon Grammar School, Ripon

Ferrari Power

F ast, furious, fierce.
E ntering another dimension.
R oaring past other cars.
R uling the road.
A voiding the large obstacles.
R overs, Nissans, no match for the Ferrari.
I gnition kicks in as the key is turned.

P ouncing through the sandy mountains.
O ver the limit.
W onderful control.
E xciting, fearless.
R uthless monster.

Tim Gilliatt (11)
Ripon Grammar School, Ripon

That's Life

Things are happening on our Earth
And new events are unfolding,
Lots of mums are giving birth
And men are putting up scaffolding.

The milkman still comes to our house
And I still go to school,
Our cat has not yet caught a mouse,
But I am still quite cool.

I play for a different footie team
And got some new teammates,
But I still can't wait 'til I'm eighteen
So I can stay out late.

However, things are still the same
And maybe they will never change,
My sister is the one I will always blame,
When milk gets spilled on the cooking range.
That's life!

Oliver Ward (12)
Ripon Grammar School, Ripon

The Sea

The sea rolls and tumbles in the night,
Carrying silent ships out of sight.
The sea washes into deep, dark caves,
Bringing seaweed and shells along in the waves.

The sea is a place where all rivers end,
They rush and they gush and they flow and they bend.
The sea is like a stormy sky,
Whose waves ripple like birds that fly.

The sea is a pool of salty tears
And is one of sailors' greatest fears.
The sea is silent, as calm as day,
The waves lap on the empty bay.

Annie Gott (12)
Ripon Grammar School, Ripon

Nocturnal Nightmares

Comes all Hallows Eve,
Mysterious, curious,
Spirits go drifting.

Ghosts scary, spooky,
Ghouls howling, terrifying,
Spectres white silent.

Haunted houses dark,
Smouldering cauldrons simmer,
Eye of toad and newt.

Empty, eerie rooms,
Flickering lights, creaking doors,
Footsteps pass on by.

Frantic howling wolves,
Hued moonlight casting shadows,
Misty graveyards cold.

Night-time hastens on,
Bewitching hours come and go,
Slowly the dawn breaks.

Katie Umpleby (12)
Ripon Grammar School, Ripon

Pandas

P eking mountains are their natural habitat
A ggressively defending their young
N ourished by bamboo shoots
D ecreasing in numbers, facing extinction
A dmirable creature - revered, holy, sacred.

Rosie Coull (12)
Ripon Grammar School, Ripon

Butterfly

An elegant beauty,
Flies from flower to flower,
Wings flapping gently,
As the wind carries it away.

A graceful flyer,
Swooping around gardens,
Brilliant colours shining,
As the wind carries it away.

A colourful insect,
Its shiny black eyes,
On its small black body,
As the wind carries it away.

A summer insect,
It may be known,
Flapping around soundlessly,
As the wind carries it away.

Laura Stockil (12)
Ripon Grammar School, Ripon

Carrots, The World's Greatest Vegetable

Oh, I do love carrots,
Much more than I can say,
Because I love my carrots,
I eat them every day.

Whether boiled or in a stew,
Whether cooked or raw,
I'll always eat my carrots,
Then I'll come and get some more.

Oh, I do love carrots,
Much more than I can say,
Because I eat my carrots,
You cannot call me gay.

Chris James (15)
Ripon Grammar School, Ripon

Death

Death is the only cert in a human's life,
Nothing can stop it, it has to arrive,
A limit worth having if only for fun,
A baby is born, the clock is ticking,
A looming presence, choking its mind,
An unstoppable occurrence for everyone to have,
But no one can say what it's like,
The effect of death affects us all,
Many don't expect it when it happens,
Love makes us cry for the deceased,
Incredible actions happen when such is achieved,
It can make life short, a quick crash of lightning,
It can make people think having avoided it for years,
It affects the richest and the poorest,
Death erupts in many different ways,
Death is the only thought that keeps us alive,
Determined to stay alive and avoid it.

Jonny Frank (14)
Ripon Grammar School, Ripon

The Measure Of A Man

The measure of a man
Is how he handles defeat
How he handles his darkest hour
Standing alone against his fear
He shouts aloud

It damages him
As he is forced to watch
His existence unravelled
His flaws exposed . . .
Oh fear is a deadly thing
But the measure of a man
Is how you handle yours.

David Harrison (15)
Ripon Grammar School, Ripon

Monday 16th August

Your glassy eyes watch me through tears,
You are a witness to my heart being bled dry,
You are a victim caught up in my pain,
Tears of emotion roll silently down your fair face.
Love the disciple of the Devil,
Satan himself inflicts this grief upon us.
The agony of love causes all reason to fade,
As we are tortured through this feeling we beg for mercy.
The fallen angel wreaks the despair of love.
Lucifer plays havoc with our feelings, our passion to cherish, desire
and dote on another,
To adore and to be adored back is chaos to our minds,
To love dooms you to your own torment.
Love is a terminal illness, everlasting in eternity.
So what do you mean when you say you love me
With tears in those glassy eyes?

Rachael Dawson (15)
Ripon Grammar School, Ripon

Memories Of School

School is waking up and realising I have to be in
school in ten minutes.
School is walking up the drive and remembering I've left my
homework on the hall table.
School is racing against the time before the bell goes.
School is forgetting to bring my books to the strictest lessons.
School is lining up in the lunch line and have everyone go
past you so you're at the end.
School is going to the 6th lesson without registration.
School is walking in the corridor underneath the bell as it goes off.
School is running through shelter as it tips with rain.
School is classroom chatter.
School is walking home through the musty allotments
smelling of stale cabbages.
School is collapsing in the car.

Poppy Bevis (11)
Ripon Grammar School, Ripon

My Pet Charlie!

He slips around the kitchen floor,
Chasing after his red rubber ball.

Scratching the door as we leave,
Seeking attention, he doesn't succeed!

Leaving surprises, disgusting and smelly,
These little things take our eyes from the telly!

Curling up in his basket, so tiny,
Chewing his toys, which were once new and shiny.

When he makes his decision to take a nap,
He waddles over to you and snuggles up on your lap!

My puppy, Charlie, isn't actually mine,
He's my brother's you see, I've been telling white lies.

My puppy, Charlie, is growing up fast,
Time has gone, time has passed.

No more games of fetch the ball,
No more scratches on the door.

All trained up, he knows the score,
He's a working Labrador!

Stephanie Lamb (11)
Ripon Grammar School, Ripon

Dead But Alive

He sits there motionless, lying in his bed.
What is wrong with him, Nurse?
Why can he not move and talk?
He did move before . . .
A loud beep sounds throughout
And the room goes
Dead.

Benjamin Crewe (11)
Ripon Grammar School, Ripon

Choices

We choose our path because there is no other choice.
God doesn't direct us, I can't hear His voice.
We are the result of the choices from the past,
Could a bad choice be our last?
The bad choices I made torment me and mankind,
It stays like a sharp splinter in my mind,
I'm influenced by my parents and teachers,
Also by evil and temptation or so the Bible preaches.
Eve bit into the fruit of truth and fate,
Suffering wickedness outside Eden's gate.
The original sin made paradise lost,
World pain and suffering is our cost.
We grow to know what's wrong and right,
The dream of world peace is so far from sight.
We can change the world, we have choice and freewill,
We can choose to make peace and love or choose to kill,
There is goodness still in the hearts of men,
Together we'll build our paradise again.

Alana Fairfax (13)
Ripon Grammar School, Ripon

Our Love . . . Is Like A Storm

Love is lightning,
Striking down,
Tears flow,
Dripping,
Slowly,
Heartbeats thump,
Like thunder,
Growling,
Always
There,
Just sometimes
Silent.

Emma Brown (11)
Ripon Grammar School, Ripon

Warning! . . . Surprised?

Look at these signs,
Are they aimed at me?
Little man, lightning strike,
What could they be?

Look at the screen,
It's a news report on TV,
Terrorists attack, we can't fight back,
This is all it ever tells me.

Look at the signpost,
'We're the safest of communities',
You will find out much later that
This has never really been.

Look at the banner
'Police line: Do not cross',
Is there any danger
Or am I the one who's dangerous?

Look, there's a war in Germany,
It's a free for all, kill 'em all,
That's all it seems to mean,
Look, there's a warning! . . . Surprised?

Sam Kirbitson (13)
Ripon Grammar School, Ripon

The Beast Of Talwar

He strikes upon the blue lit moon,
His crooked hands and razor-sharp claws gleam
With the lightness of the stars,
His twisted, but pointed fangs ready to sink into his prey,
His eyes are as red as the fresh blood of a human,
He's ready, are you?

Noel Edwards (13)
Ripon Grammar School, Ripon

Love Is . . .

Love is like a red balloon,
Love is the makings of your life,
Love is sometimes a scare from behind,
Love is . . .

Love is as hot as a beach in summer,
Love is cold like a white snow angel,
Love is what makes the world spin,
Love is . . .

Love is like the world around us,
Love is a haven in the darkest alleys,
Love is a fire on a cold winter's night,
Love is . . .

Love is the glow of a sixty-watt bulb,
Love is the light of a thousand candles,
Love is what fills the hole in my heart,
Love is . . .

Paul Heath-Smith (13)
Ripon Grammar School, Ripon

Tiger

Faster and faster in the black of night,
Almost flying through the grass.
As silent as a sleeping mouse,
Stalking slowly through the silence.
Hunting its unlucky prey.
Getting quicker, getting fast,
Hoping that the chase won't last.
Then it's stopped like a storm,
First it thunders, then it's gone.
Just like a flash of light,
There wasn't even
A fight.

Jonathan Green (13)
Ripon Grammar School, Ripon

What Is Lime?

What is lime?
Lime is a forgotten dream that got lost in time,
A petrified child having all the things they have ever known
Stripped away from them,
Lime is all the mistakes you've ever made,
Memories that will never fade.

Lime is darkness,
A tumultuous growl,
A cold killer on the prowl,
Lime is the first plant dying in winter.

Lime is being blinded by the light,
Getting yourself into a fight,
Lime is a feeling that is hard to explain,
That appears happy but is hurting inside,
It's being swept away by the tide,
That is life.

Lime is a stark reminder that our world is not perfect,
Brutal animals go around causing destruction,
Not bothered by the effect,
But what is a world without lime?

Sarah Fortune (12)
Ripon Grammar School, Ripon

The Apparition

Slim, dark, he walked through the night
Holding an axe as he looked left and right
I hid in the shadows and watched as he passed
His breath hit me with an icy blast
He looked my way with a vacant stare
And simply vanished into thin air.

Sam Coles (13)
Ripon Grammar School, Ripon

The Birth Of A Terrorist

Over a perfect child
Proud parents grin.
Every inch a unique part
Of purity, without sin.

Patterns in the iris of an eye,
Swirls on the tip of a finger.
A mother wants to stay forever,
Just to watch, just to linger.

The grasp of a tiny hand,
The scent of smooth warm skin.
A first enchanting smile,
A family's next of kin.

Life unfolds predictably
Like the petals of a rose,
Until sowed are the seeds of evil,
By humanity's true foes.

A once blank canvas of perfection,
Now shattered with evil slivers
A meticulous explosion of thought,
And faith in mankind quivers.

With each new day comes lifesaving cures,
A world of knowledge, of careful construction.
In unclean hands this knowledge gives birth to
A child of power, of terrorising destruction.

Over a perfect child
Proud parents grin.
Every inch a unique part
Of purity, without sin.

Rebecca Dobbins (16)
Ripon Grammar School, Ripon

Little Word

He said, 'No'
And it may be a small and
Inconspicuous word,
But it has significance and
Status.
It takes little effort to have it
Flow out of your mouth, but has a
Major effect.
I am not a victim of the word 'no',
Still I am not a winner
I have not gained
Riches or glory from it
Nor have I been looked down upon
Yet as that little word hit me
I was immediately deprived
I was knocked down by the force and
Strength of it
Just one little word
And it may seem to you that
It has little power
But I will probably
Never forget
The time he said
'No.'

Benedict Clancy (13)
Ripon Grammar School, Ripon

Statue Of Liberty On September 11th

A dust rises over my city,
As crashes are heard.
My city is silenced,
Shocked and frightened.

The siren is heard,
There is something wrong,
More sirens pass by,
But I cannot see for the dusty sky.

As the dust settles,
My skyline misses,
Something most precious,
My people are anxious.

My people still mourn,
For all that is lost.
My towers are gone,
But we will still fight on.

I am a symbol of liberty,
But how can it be,
That these people are free?

Jacob Clolinger (13)
Ripon Grammar School, Ripon

A Leaf In The Eyes Of . . .

Crisp, crumbly, as dry as rock,
Soft, delicate,
Gentle as candyfloss,
Lonely, secluded, all alone,
Trodden on, stamped across,
No one gives a toss!

Maria DeMartino (14)
Ripon Grammar School, Ripon

The Beach

The sweeping sands rush by in the evening breeze,
The sea at peace with the world at last,
A romantic sunset closes the day,
Yet a young couple still take a stroll,
Seizing every moment of a wonderland walk.

Early in the morning the sun breaks free,
A sheet of red pulled across the sky,
An empty beach, no lights, no sound,
The town awakes from an eternal sleep,
Harmony will last not a moment longer.

Later on, the beach is crowded, laughter in the air,
Happy holidaymakers licking ice cream,
The hot sun beats down on the warm golden sand,
Children swim amongst the waves,
The beach is booming full of families.

Matthew Garner (12)
Ripon Grammar School, Ripon

4.10am Heathrow

Early morning mists still rising,
grassy plains outline the path.
Dark grey skies loom down,
seeing the terminal in the distance.
Pause,
then as the arrow leaves the bow.
Fire escapes the prison of the engine,
throwing max power.
Nose going up to face the deadly climb.
Higher,
    higher.
       Reaching up
          through the
             blanket of dirt
                and cotton.

Michael Gilbert (11)
Ripon Grammar School, Ripon

What Happened? Where Did It Go?

The bright and breezy spring,
Waiting for new life to begin.
What happened?
Where did it go?

The warm and sunny summer,
A buzzy bee, a hummer.
What happened?
Where did it go?

The golden and shiny autumn,
Waiting for winter to summon.
What happened?
Where did it go?

The white and snowy winter,
My knees start to jitter.
What happened?
Where did it go?

Morgan Brice (11)
Ripon Grammar School, Ripon

What's Passion?

It's the happiness when you're sad
The friend when you're alone
The bright light in the darkness
It creeps up on you like a cheetah
Waiting to feed its hunger
It's the child tickling you from inside
It's the knot you feel being weaved and twisted
Like a spider preparing its web
The splash of colour on a white canvas
It's the flash car driving all motivation
The security guard to your soul
Gold is passion and passion is golden
You are the passion which nurses the world.

Olivia Bowden (12)
Ripon Grammar School, Ripon

Night

Night is the time when it's silent,
Night is the time when nobody stirs,
Night is the time when the stars light up the sky,
Night is . . .

Night is when you drift off to sleep,
Night is when the clouds hang high,
Night is when the moon shines bright,
Night is . . .

Night is when your night light flickers,
Night is when shadows creep around,
Night is when dreams swirl in your head,
Night is . . .

Night is when your fears unfold,
Night is when bats scream and cry,
Night is when darkness spreads around,
Night is . . .

Kate Gatford (12)
Ripon Grammar School, Ripon

Desert Jungle

D esert lands, barren and wasted
E verything gone, destroyed and abandoned
S trange plants, animals and places
E very town, village and farm left
R olling sand dunes in every direction
T orrential rain falling heavily

J ungle storms thunder and lightning
U nderneath the canopy of leaves
N o light reached the jungle floor
G rowing life feasting on the rain
L onely animals wandering around
E verything silent, sill, unmoving.

James Everett (12)
Ripon Grammar School, Ripon

The Game

The sky is all still red
From the blood I had to spill
Everything is grey
Everything is still

I surrender to the silent screams
That echo all around
I feel like I am floating
But my feet stay on the ground

The tears are flowing everywhere
Swallowing me whole
They're engulfing both my lungs
Trying to wash away my soul

My mind is so disturbed
That I can't tell what is real
The emotions that I used to know
I no longer feel

All I know is misery
All I know is pain
All I know is death
And that life is one cruel game.

Nadia Smith (14)
Ripon Grammar School, Ripon

Through The Window

Sun shining, trees swaying,
Flowers blossoming, birds flying,
Clouds gliding, bees buzzing,
Outside on a beautiful summer's day.

Rain cascading, leaves tumbling,
Conkers smashing, wind gushing,
Branches snapping, mist blinding,
Outside on a breezy autumn day.

Snow falling, flakes swirling,
Clouds glowing, rivers freezing,
Cold biting, children sledging,
Outside on a crisp winter's day.

Sky brightening, streams flowing,
Bulbs opening, lambs bleating,
Clouds whitening, farmers ploughing,
Outside on a refreshing spring day.

Sun shining, birds flying,
Rain cascading, snow falling,
Cold biting, sky brightening,
Outside as the seasons revolve.

Laura Gilbert (14)
Ripon Grammar School, Ripon

The Whispering Of The Parting

Do you know me?
Do you hear me?
I used to live here
But I died last year.
Do you care for me?
Do you recognise me?
You used to love me
But you do no more
Have you seen me?
Would you die for me?
Do you really know me?
Do you weep for me?
Is your heart deep with me?
Do you feel what I feel?
Do you think you know pain?
How about the pain you gave me?
As I felt you piercing my skin
With your harsh words
I still remember the day
You promised me the world
And the next day
You killed me.

Rebecca Davies (11)
Ripon Grammar School, Ripon

Happiness Is . . .

Happiness is a cup of hot chocolate on a cold winter's day,
Happiness is the splash at the bottom of a slide,
Happiness is the feel of money in your hand,
Happiness is . . .

Happiness is children playing in the sun,
Happiness is building an ice-cold snowman,
Happiness is the warmth of ocean-side sand,
Happiness is . . .

Happiness is all the flavours in the ice cream shop,
Happiness is the sugar in a cup of tea,
Happiness is salmon jumping through a waterfall,
Happiness is . . .

Happiness is the smell of burning pine cones,
Happiness is the smell after rain,
Happiness is popping bubble wrap with your feet,
Happiness is . . .

Happiness is a hug between good friends,
Happiness is reading a really good book,
Happiness is being with your family,
Happiness is . . .

Rebecca Ellis (13)
Ripon Grammar School, Ripon

Life Is . . .

Life is the feeling of waking up,
Life is having great mates,
Life is going on holiday,
Life is . . .

Life is the annoyance of having an enemy,
Life is the pain of starting to die,
Life is starting to get old,
Life is . . .

Life is watching a fun programme,
Life is reading an award-winning book,
Life is being young,
Life is . . .

Life is losing a sense,
Life is unfair,
Life is life,
Life is . . .

George Dobbins (12)
Ripon Grammar School, Ripon

Feelings

A clash of feeling,
A deadly mix,
Your life is haunted by the risk.
You never know your next attack -
As calm as time?
A stamping bull?
The future is so strange!

You'll end up hurt
If you let them get the best of you
But be careful how you use them
They are not always true

So keep a careful, wary eye
Feelings pass and time flies by.

Katy Gears (13)
Ripon Grammar School, Ripon

Night Is . . .

Night is dark,
Night is dreams,
Night is when nothing is what it seems.
Night is a shadow, creeping round a room,
Night has a sense of increasing gloom.
Night is the moon,
Night is a star,
Night is so dark you've no idea where you are.
Night is the story before you go to bed,
Night is when you rest your head.
Night is silence
And your darkest fear,
When all you want is someone near.
Night is a nightmare, the thing you hate,
Night is when you stay up really late.
Night is endless,
Like a deep black hole,
Night is black,
Like a piece of coal.
Night is . . .

Naomi Fowler (12)
Ripon Grammar School, Ripon

Alone - Haiku

Silence, loneliness,
The hermit will live and die,
Away from the world.

Daniel Lee (14)
Ripon Grammar School, Ripon

My School . . .

My school is very well run
My school is an awful lot of fun
My school shines under the lovely sun

My school . . .

My school is really great
My school is running excited through the gate
My school is fun at break
My school is playing with my mates

My school . . .

My school is watching the football
My school is filled with people big and small
My school is unbelievably *cool!*

My school . . .

George Bevington (11)
Ripon Grammar School, Ripon

Time

An everlasting course of tackling the world,
In millions of tiny forms its shape is taken.
It hijacks youth far too quickly,
It demolishes cities, ruins empires
And brings on death.
It's a secret organisation running your life.
Every minute computed,
Every second followed.
A depending source that never runs out,
A lifelong item that keeps on living.
Sealed and contained secretly in a clock,
Time never ever breaks free.

Charlotte Ellerby (12)
Ripon Grammar School, Ripon

Rivers

Gushing, ravenous beast,
swallowing everything up,
everything is hidden,
        out
          of
           sight,
a fathomless ghost in the dead of night,
flooding silently,
        engulfing
           everything
from the mysterious depths it strikes.
Up in the peaceful mountains,
a little stream is born,
no one knows the destruction
          it
            will
              cause.
Monsters lurking in the
        deep,
        dark
        depths.

Rochyne Delaney McNulty (12)
Ripon Grammar School, Ripon

Sharks

Murky shadow under the waves searching through
The death-black eyes.
Closing in on the bait, swift ripples towards the struggle of the legs.
Bursting through the surface, diving on its prey.
Then the splashes of the legs dying.
The pool of blood rising and floating
And then the creature retreats waiting for its next strike.

Daniel Hunt (12)
Ripon Grammar School, Ripon

Clouds

Floating in the bright blue sky,
Dancing graciously way up high,
Soft and fluffy like a teddy bear,
Hovering simply without a care.

A glisten of sunlight on its face,
Then suddenly it's gone without a trace,
Carried along by such a force,
Taking a whooshing obstacle course.

It's changing colour from a white to a grey,
Now it feels like night, not day,
There's a rumble of thunder and a downpour of rain
And a crash and a bang and a sound of pain.

Rain pelting down from the black-rimmed cloud,
The thunder and lightning, oh they're so loud,
Still being dragged through the darkened sky,
Over the rooftops and buildings they fly.

After a while there's a spot of blue sky
And a fluffy white cloud floats past, way up high,
The wind has changed; I've got nothing to fear,
The storm has gone and summer is here!

Harriert Floyd (13)
Ripon Grammar School, Ripon

The Unpredictable Element

It never stops to let you think,
It flies straight by you when having fun.
There is never enough of it to make that crucial link.
You have to make it to get the job done.

There is never enough of it
And yet there is too much of it.
It passes you by too quickly
And yet too slowly.

You wish you had more of it in order to understand,
You wish to reverse it, to set things straight.
You can save it by dismissing the matter at hand,
It always has a means of making you late.

There is never enough of it
And yet too much of it.
It passes you by too quickly
And yet too slowly.

It is indeed quite an unpredictable element,
It is one that should be made the most of,
Because it is one you can later repent,
For one day you will ask yourself,

Was my time well spent?

Kieran Anderson (14)
Ripon Grammar School, Ripon

A Journey To The City!

Slowly the train starts to crawl,
Away from the crumbling village walls.
Past the massive towers
And the blooming flowers.

The train speeds up,
In the lady's hand there's a shaking cup.
The train turns right
And over the hill there's a glimmer of light.

Closer, closer,
Towards the city,
Closer, closer,
Towards the city.

Faster, faster,
Towards the city.
Faster, faster
Towards the city.

All the children are now asleep
Not even a single peep.
The train again starts to crawl
And a single child starts to bawl.

We're nearly there,
The city's ahead.
We're nearly there,
The city's ahead.

Here we are,
The city's here.
Here we are,
The city's here.

Katie Davill (12)
Ripon Grammar School, Ripon

When I Think Of Home I Hear . . .

When I think of home,
I hear
Birdsong,
Door creaking, water washing,
Tap dripping.
Plimp . . . plimp . . . plimp.
Click and scrape of brother's Lego,
Elephant footsteps galumph downstairs,
Crunch of breakfast toast.
Getting dressed reveals havoc.
'Mum, have you washed any socks for me?'
A scrabble for toys comes from the wardrobe,
Turning pages from reading books.
Ghostly whispers, happy laughter,
Babbling voices.
Shouting parents, whimpering children,
Stamping feet, slamming doors.
Tap dancing computer keys.
Ticking of clocks as hours go by,
Tick, tick, tick, tick.
Glugging milk, scrubbing brush,
Pearly white gnashing teeth.
Rustling of duvet, like folding newspaper.
Whispers of blessings before sleep, like a cool
Cold wind through trees.
Fading footsteps . . . silence . . . owl shrieks . . . silence.

Bryony Gillespie (12)
Ryedale School, York

When I Think Of Rievaulx Stables I Hear . . .

When I think of Rievaulx Stables I hear . . .
Loud neighs coming from the impatient horses,
Then as loud as a lion roaring I hear . . .
The sound of a slammed door
And just then as the stables go quiet,
The silence gets broken,
By the sound of shovels on the concrete floor.
In the stable there's a noise of brushes sweeping,
As mice scuttle across the hay barn,
As quiet as a scribbling pen,
A metal bucket screeching,
As loud as an angry eagle in the distance
And then,
A final sound of horses settling down,
Munching quietly on their hay,
All the noises settle just before another loud day.

Amy Collier (11)
Ryedale School, York

What Am I?

I'm a
Fun maker
A mum upsetter
A white coat
A road hazard
A job for gritters
A chilly touch
A soggy mess
A downhill ride
A freezing fighter
And a chilly shiver up your spine

What am I?
The snow.

Charlotte Fairweather (11)
Ryedale School, York

A Cold Day

Icicles on the garage stuck,
Frost on the grass shivers to the morning,
A blanket of shade covers the ground,
The smoke from the exhaust floats,
To the chilly air within.

Child coughs and blows its nose
And hurries to the car warm,
But then, as it has never seemed to occur,
A bird sings.

The window glows a warm light
And inside the most beautiful tree
That the world has ever seen
And under, wrapped boxes lay.

Above the sky turns grey
And robins go to their homes.
Suddenly white dots soon appear
And cover the grass in a mist of white.
The child appears and dances on the ground
And cries, 'Snow!'

Ruby Williams (11)
Ryedale School, York

When I Think Of Home I Hear . . .

When I think of home I hear . . .
Dogs barking,
Mum shouting,
Cooker's humming like a swarm of bees.
A roar of anger,
Owls hooting, like a steam train about to depart.
The sound of a boiler at 6am,
Cows bellowing in the fields nearby.
The sound of the frog fountain, like a trickling brook
And then buzz, the alarm at 6.45.

Alistair Holmes (11)
Ryedale School, York

What Am I?

I'm a
Bib dribbler
A toy chewer
A nappy wetter
A crying crackpot
A mushy food eater
A potty number twoer
A milk-drinking catastrophe
I'm a
King of the sleeps, toilets and tantrums,
A major, major mistake,
A grumpy little so and so,
What am I?
A baby.

Robert Thurlow (11)
Ryedale School, York

What Am I?

I'm a
Oily pot,
A rubber burner,
As fast as the wind,
A zooming antelope,
But not as fast,
Going at the speed limit.

Just slowing down,
At the right pace,
I didn't get a ticket,
What a relief!
But been warned
And not been charged,
What a wonderful day!

Suzanne Jefferson (11)
Ryedale School, York

What Am I?

I'm a
Skin scorcher
A happy holidaymaker
A face of sweat
A flower opener
A lollipop dripper
A big smile on your face
I'm an early riser
And a late setter
A farmer's delight
But a snowman's worst fear
A glittering light for the world

What am I?
The sun.

Charlotte Collier (11)
Ryedale School, York

What Am I?

I am a . . .
Teleporter into faraway lands
A sack of coal
A feather
A bore
A waste of space
An image
Yet just a couple of ideas spotted with
Imagination
What am I?

A book.

Louise Smith (11)
Ryedale School, York

Tree

The tree is a waving grandpa
Saying *goodbye my grandchild*
And now, the sweeties come pouring from his clothes
Onto the ground below
He invites you to sit upon his knee
In his old and withered arms
And climbs up and around his shoulders
To hide from the world beyond.

Philippa Adderley (11)
Ryedale School, York

What Am I?

I'm a
Nose chiller
A scarf knotter
A tree coverer
A fantastic thing for making figures
White dust on the ground
Melting when the sun comes out

What am I?
The snow.

Christie Hewitt (11)
Ryedale School, York

Homophone Poem

As wee walked into hour class today,
Eye sat and red and began two say,
'Excuse me Miss, it's ate past too
And today is the day hour test is dew.
Wee knead two go now, wee cannot bee late,
Four anytime now, it'll bee too past ate!
Eye have too go now, because eye am the best
And eye cannot bare too miss even won test!'

Rufus Brooks (12)
Ryedale School, York

When I Think Of Shooting I Hear . . .

When I think of shooting
I hear . . .
Cursing of shooters
Rushing of beaters' feet in the cornfield, lost
Crunch of leaves, echoing
Then a wild flap of wings
Bang, crack, bang, bang . . .

Then guns close, snap
Once more *bang, bang, fiercely*
Clamber, squelch, clamber, squelch
High remarks tossed
The squelch of mud on wellies moving . . .

Jonny Pattenden (11)
Ryedale School, York

The Phantom

The fog is a *creepy* phantom
Crawling silently up the street
His cloudy figure hogs the sky
Waiting anxiously for something to meet

His *spooky* face glares down the alley
He hovers close to the ground
He fills the alley full of cloud
He whistles but there's no sound

He turns his misty head
And transforms the blue to white
His ghostly face fills the air
The *mysterious* spirit of day and night.

Phoebe Maxwell (11)
Ryedale School, York

What Am I?

I'm a
Cat scarer,
A neighbour annoyer,
I'm a playful pal,
A homework eater,
I'm a fearless hunter,
A sofa destroyer,
I'm a hairy stinker
A man's best friend

What am I?
A puppy.

Jimmy Goode (11)
Ryedale School, York

What Am I?

I'm a
Cheese muncher
A cat teaser under their feet
A small scuttler like a bug
Pink nose
White whiskers like snow
Beady eyes, black as night
A playful pal
A sniffer for food
A hole in the skirting board
And through I pop
But then a snap, a small trap
I run and scuttle everywhere.
What am I?
A mouse.

Antonia Clark (11)
Ryedale School, York

The Stars

The stars are glittering jewels,
Studded on the sky,
Like guiding lamps against black velvet,
Twinkling by and by.

The stars are glittering jewels,
Studded on the sky,
Like silver sparks on an inky spill,
Gleaming way up high.

The stars were glittering jewels,
Studded on the sky,
But then they turned and walked away,
Fading till they died.

Rosie Hayman (11)
Ryedale School, York

What Am I?

I'm an
Orange ball
A tan machine
A stream evaporator
A tumble-dryer
A grass fader
A plant bloomer
I rise and shine
Don't look me in the face
What am I?
The sun.

Heather Weston (11)
Ryedale School, York

When I Think Of Home I Hear . . .

When I think of home I hear . . .
Trees swaying, their leaves rustling like copper pennies.
Tractor engines buzzing like tigers roaring.
Above that comes the noise of neighbours shouting,
Voices greeting passers-by.
Dogs start barking, the letterbox rattles as the post drops through.
Then I can hear the cockerel crowing, doesn't he know it's
half-past ten?
In the distance guns shoot, pheasants squawk in fright.
Clocks tick all through the house, they chime eight o'clock,
The owls hoot, *tu-whit, tu-whoo,* as if they know the night is upon us.

Elisa Caton (11)
Ryedale School, York

What Am I?

I'm a . . .
Holidaymaker,
Smile bringer,
Sand warmer,
Towel drier,
Ice cream melter,
Shadow stretcher,
But I'll never go away,
Not unless you stop smiling.
The sun.

Meg Holmes (11)
Ryedale School, York

What Am I?

I am a skin burner
A tree feeder
A blazing light
A lotion user
A faraway star
An outside radiator
Warmth like a loving hug
A huge torch
I am blinding if you look at me
The sun.

Emma Bumby (11)
Ryedale School, York

When I Think Of The Countryside I See . . .

When I think of the countryside I see
Fields as neat as patchwork
Impatient leaves pushing and shoving like football players
Clouds flying in the sky like ballet dancers
Grass waves in the breeze
Birds swooping, hovering and diving
A rainbow fading like an out-dated billboard in the sky
Then I see the sun descending . . .
Then disappearing.

Gail Humpleby (11)
Ryedale School, York

Cold Day

Puffed snow blankets the town,
Windswept, powdery. A face slapped with cold appears
In hazy telescopes of the eyes,
It begins to form a man from the iced covering,
The iced covering chokes on white, frosty
Tobacco in a harsh pipe.
No birds sing, save a solitary robin.
'Has the white time come?' he asks.
Indeed it has. Normal pipes are smoked by mouths
In swaddled scarves.
The man is made, smokes *his* borrowed pipe.
He watches stairways,
Sharp railings, black tarred, succumb to ice, long as the liar's nose.
White-crystalled diamonds glint in wandering winds
Forcing on wool lump sweaters
Sent from elderly relations
This time last year.
A sky clock ticks, the redbreast hops
And death, his warm self, smoking a pipe of mystery and fear,
Takes the ever-watching man.
Silence. He silently dies.

Alert, black trees sprout shots of farewells,
Greenness.
Goodnight winter.
It was a cold day.

Harry Wright (11)
Ryedale School, York

When I Think Of The Seaside I Hear . . .

The scurry of the worried crabs
The bustle of the gift shop bags
The squawk of seagulls swooping low
The children shouting, *'Go! Go! Go!'*
The peaceful sway of the sea
The powerful sting of the bumblebee
Many shouts are heard down low
As far as bubbling fishes go
The crunch of sand like crocodiles' jaws
The pad of puppies' bumbling paws
The babble of laughter shining around
The hooves of stressed donkeys flatten the ground.

Megan Brown (11)
Ryedale School, York

Autumn Sunshine

The sun in autumn,
Glitters bright,
The moon in autumn,
Sparkles all night.

Dew in autumn,
Leaves moist ground,
Dew in autumn,
Doesn't make a sound.

Birds sing,
While sun rises.
It's a new day,
With new surprises.

Bryony Watson (11)
St Mary's Catholic High School, Grimsby

Drowned Sorrows

It was a cold and windy day,
Oh how I wished it wouldn't rain.
I brushed the leaves from off my feet,
A single tear fell down my cheek.

I walked through the park and sat down on a bench,
Looking up at the trees my fingers clench.
I loved you and thought you loved me,
But I was wrong it would never be.

Now you're with her and I'm all alone,
Our house is empty, there's no one at home.
Then I realised what I could do,
To show how much I loved you.

The river's deep,
The water's calm.
No more heartache,
No more harm.

Nichola Robinson (13)
St Mary's Catholic High School, Grimsby

Secondary School

Stepping out of one world,
Into another,
Never knowing what's around the corner,
Apprehensive thoughts flowing around my mind,
Like an ocean,
Danger, excitement,
Who knows what is coming?
All a mist of the distant future,
A relighting candle,
An everlasting adventure.

Mollie Robertson (11)
St Mary's Catholic High School, Grimsby

Oh Dear!

Yesterday we made scones, Dear,
Today we're making bread.
Instructions in that book, Dear,
That book you should have read.

A big bowl in that cupboard, Dear,
A sharp knife in that drawer.
One tablespoon of yeast, Dear,
One tablespoon times four.

Put it in the oven, Dear,
Give it time to cook.
Leave it for a while, Dear,
Then take a sneaky look.

Take it out of the oven, Dear,
Wear your oven glove.
Time for us to taste it,
The part that we all love!

Leanne Fothergill (12)
St Mary's Catholic High School, Grimsby

Autumn Is Here

The trees become bare, as the wind
Whistles and whirls around,
Buckets falling down and down,
The roar of the wind and the swaying of the trees,
A pool of colours lay still on the ground,
All the soft, silky and slippery
Colours of autumn are finally here,
A grey dirty cloth lays over the sky,
Squirrels collect nuts as winter lays ahead.

Charlotte Rogers (11)
St Mary's Catholic High School, Grimsby

My Favourite Pizza

I'm making a pizza the size of the sun,
a pizza that'll weigh more than a ton,
a pizza too massive to pick up and toss,
a pizza filled with gallons of sauce.

I'm topping my pizza with mountains of cheese,
with acres of peppers, pineapple and peas,
with mushrooms, tomatoes, sausages and more,
with every last olive they had at the store.

My pizza is sure to be one of a kind,
my pizza will leave all others behind,
my pizza will be a wonderful treat
and all who love pizza are welcome to eat.

Tom Pell (12)
St Mary's Catholic High School, Grimsby

My Happy Feeling

My colour is yellow like the bright sun
It tastes of fruit water in the afternoon
It smells of cooked dinner on a Wednesday
Sounds like birds singing and sometimes quiet
It feels warm, great and makes me feel good.

Chris Goodier (14)
The Forest School, Knaresborough

My Emotion

My colour of emotion is very bright and breezy
It tastes like cooking apples
It smells like chocolate sauce
It looks like
Chocolaty-brown and gooey
It sounds like a train running.

Kyle Watson (12)
The Forest School, Knaresborough

Happy Feeling

I feel happy my colour is red and black
It tasted like a sausage running away
It smelt like a rolling away football
It sounds like a funny pop group called Busted
It felt like a big, messy, horrible, nasty bedroom.

Michael Riley
The Forest School, Knaresborough

Bright And Breezy

My colour of emotion is
very bright and breezy
My emotion tastes like
cooking apples and chocolate sauce
My emotion looks brown
and gooey
It sounds like a train
running by.

Isobel Chapman (13)
The Forest School, Knaresborough

Poetry

My colour is happy as lilac
As pink as a rose perfume
Scented like a daffodil
Juicy as an apple
Romantic as a love heart
Really cuddly and soft
I love lilac because it makes me feel happy
I like pink because it looks like a beautiful rose.

Jessica Gregory
The Forest School, Knaresborough

Candyfloss

My colour is pink
It tastes like candyfloss
And smells like roses
It looks like fluffy clouds
It sounds like music to my ears
It feels like soft cotton wool
With a sugary coating.

Amy Marshall
The Forest School, Knaresborough

Happiness

When I am happy
My world is green like a lawn
It tastes like an apple
But smells like a rose
It looks like a star that is twinkling bright
And sounds like giggling
Which makes me feel bubbly and light.

Alice Watson (13)
The Forest School, Knaresborough

Pancakes

One special week on a Tuesday, pancake day
It's in one exciting month but not in May
March is the day you need eggs, butter and flour
If you don't put these in, it'll taste sour
On top treacle, sugar, lemon and honey
I could make lots of money with my pancakes
Or maybe I'll eat them and have breakfast in bed.

Suzanne Greenbeck (11)
Tollbar Business & Enterprise College, Grimsby

Ghosts!

On Ghost Island I can see,
Tiny ghosts looking at me
With their tiny faces
And their wide eyes,
Green and yellow,
Looking like pies!
I started to run,
I started to cry,
Then I stopped
And thought, why?
They won't hurt me,
They won't touch me,
Then again,
Ghosts are creepy!

Millie Dowie (12)
Tollbar Business & Enterprise College, Grimsby

Oozing Island

First of all it was dark,
I couldn't find a camper park,
I found some caves but they were damp,
They laid down just to camp.
In the morning it was cold,
Sometimes I wish that I was sold,
To my Shaun he is warm,
The next morning, it was windy,
Sometimes I wish for my doll called Cindy.
Goodbye to my deserted island,
On the radio it's Barbara Streisand.

Annaliese York (12)
Tollbar Business & Enterprise College, Grimsby

Life In The Trenches

The fear, the death
It sounds like Macbeth
The blood, the guts
The half-broken huts
The stink, the smell
They've gone through hell
The bombs, oh why
The thick smoky sky
The guns and bangs
Can only mean we are in no-man's-land

The holes in the ground
The high-pitched sounds
The sweat and tears
Comes within all our fears
We cry, sob and weep
But try not to make a peep
For night is coming with sounds of a band
For we are still stuck in no-man's-land.

Sophie Gowan (13)
Tollbar Business & Enterprise College, Grimsby

World War I Poetry

The smell in the trenches,
Rotting flesh off the soldiers who died,
The disgusting smell of the rats,
Dampness in the trench.

The sounds of the bombs thundering down,
Machine guns rattling while the bullets fire out,
The sound of death
And people's screams.

In the trenches I see people injured
And dying,
The huge bombs flying over,
To each enemy's side.

Danny Bacon (13)
Tollbar Business & Enterprise College, Grimsby

Dreamy Island

B ig volcanoes towering high,
E very detail counts,
A mystery cave in the gloom,
U tterly beautiful,
T he mermaids singing in the sun,
Y ou will never know what hit you

M ountains
E motions
R abbit corners
M arshmallow volcano
A mystery
I ndispicable
D angerous journey
S and

C oves
A dventures
V ictims to its wail
E atable treats
S un.

Alice Sykes (12)
Tollbar Business & Enterprise College, Grimsby

Chewing Gum

Never put your hand under the table,
There are things that are very stable,
If you accidentally do,
You may feel very new,
Under the table is something yum,
Because believe it or not, it's *chewing gum!*
There are many flavours under there,
Some you might think are a nightmare,
Now you know what to do,
Just reach down under and have a chew.

Alexandra Thomas (11)
Tollbar Business & Enterprise College, Grimsby

Noises At Night

Every night I go to bed
But my sister and brother are
Still silly in the head
My sister's music's on
And brothers are chewing chewing gum
These nights are all the same
First my mum's car won't start
And she is going crazy again
She's pulling out her hair
And bawling and shouting
And I think the only time she's going to stop
Is when she finally bursts
Dad's just saying, 'Calm down
It's not that bad'
And off she goes again
It's the worst that could happen
I'm going to be late for work
My sister's shouting from upstairs
'Shut up, shut up right now!'
And Dad finally puts the music on
(The good music.)

Lucy Dean (11)
Tollbar Business & Enterprise College, Grimsby

The Island Poem

The huge wave rolling into the shore
Bringing sand and pebbles
Sun shining, the wind blowing the palm trees
Moving the leaves in funny patterns
Clouds move in the air slowly, white and puffy
They are there watching you all the time
The island is deserted, no one is there . . .
Except you and the ghost of Blair.

Liam Chalder (13)
Tollbar Business & Enterprise College, Grimsby

A Cheeky Little Monkey

I went to the jungle on a bright sunny day
I saw lots of animals they came out to play
There was one in particular I couldn't forget
A cheeky little monkey was a cheeky little threat

He had lots of fun swinging tree to tree
Grabbing bananas, throwing them at me
He thought it was funny, he thought it was a laugh
The animals took sides with him even the giraffe

I started to get tired, so I slowly fell asleep
I just started to dream, when I heard a little beep
So I opened up my eyes, but was this place in my head?
I quickly sat up and realised I was in my bed!

Shannon Bradley (11)
Tollbar Business & Enterprise College, Grimsby

Come On You Spurs!

Tottenham are the best,
They're better than the rest,
We hate Arsenal, yes we do,
And West Ham too!

We've got Jermain,
Teams call him a pain,
Cos when he gets the ball,
He scores a *goal!*

'Come on you Spurs,'
All the fans sing,
As well as that,
We have Ledley King!

So come on you Spurs,
Win it for us,
We are the best
And no one can beat us!

Shaun Moughton (12)
Tollbar Business & Enterprise College, Grimsby

It's Wintertime!

It's wintertime,
It's wintertime,
The ground is filled with snow,
Look at the Christmas trees,
Look at the baubles glow;
Sh, sh, Father Christmas is coming,
Can you hear the angels humming?
Look at the presents under the tree,
I wonder is there any for me?
No, no, there is none,
Father Christmas has now gone,
I wonder why! I wonder why!
All that's left is an apple pie,
Was it Mum or was it Dad?
Now I am feeling so very sad.

Kelly Winn (12)
Tollbar Business & Enterprise College, Grimsby

Winter

First day of winter, there's lots of snow
Wrap up warm and away we go

Wake up in the morning and see a blanket of ice
When we're all snuggled up in bed like newborn mice

Wrapped up in my warm woolly coat
Which cost my mum a few pound notes

Looking for slopes, me and my sledge
Gone too fast, straight through a hedge!

It's cold outside, my cheeks rosy and red
Pleased I've got my big woolly hat on my head

Can't wait for summer to come
Lots of fun and a big bright sun!

Eleanor Devonport (12)
Tollbar Business & Enterprise College, Grimsby

War Poem

Maconochie, pea soup and many calories a day,
Bully beef, biscuits and emergency food,
Rum, cold food and horsemeat lumps.

Bad conditions, rarely above sea level.
Waterlogged with rain and collapsing sides,
German advantage, duckboards and trench foot.

Infected, numb, red or blue feet.
Amputation, whale oil grease and three pairs of socks,
Gangrenous, untreated trench foot.

Swarming, running, stripping off flesh,
Large, bold, taking from the dead.
Found in groups, going into eyes.

Blighty wounds, shooting themselves,
Suicide, rifles pressed against heads.
Enemy snipers, triggers and offences.

Calvary, motor vehicles, horses and mules,
Squadrons, rough rides and dismounting,
Sawdust cakes, horses killed and wounded.

Sour and stale smells, delousing machines,
Frenzied scratching and disease,
Pyrexia and trench fever.

Stomach pains, diarrhoea and vomiting,
Fever-infected people, no proper sanitation,
Contaminated water, chloride of lime.

Food, trench life, trench foot and rats,
Self-inflicted wounds, horses and mules.
Body lice and dysentery.

All these are what I remember about the war.
I know there's something I've forgotten,
Death.

Rebecca Caroline (13)
Tollbar Business & Enterprise College, Grimsby

We Are Town!

We are Town
We are not going down
We're the best
Forget all the rest
Because here comes Town

There was a man named Sestanovich
He is the star player on the pitch
He does his tricks
Then scores six
Because everyone loves him

Grimsby Town all the way
I don't care what people say
We are cool
The other team drool
Because we are Town!

GTFC
We've got a sting like a bee
Can you hear the pontoon knights
Underneath the big floodlights
We are proud
We are loud
GTFC.

Adelé Douthwaite (12)
Tollbar Business & Enterprise College, Grimsby

Going Over The Top

In this horrid trench I lay
Hoping the shells won't hit me
Crashing as loud as thunder
The noise is deafening
We have to move corpses asunder

A whistle blows as the noise stops
I grab my gun and
Get ready to go over the top

Everywhere I look
There is a crater or a dead man
I see a flashing light
Hear an explosion
And feel pain in my arm

And another in my leg
Again in my chest
As I hit the ground
The pain goes away
All I can see goes black

All this war has caused is
Anger, hatred and pain
As I die, I think of two words:
Never again.

Matty Everard (13)
Tollbar Business & Enterprise College, Grimsby

The Last Day, The Only Day

Another day is over
I'm still here
The darkness is creeping
From the corners of the Earth
I can see a face
A man I killed today
It's like the world is woven with dark lace

I lay in my bunk listening
I hear the beat of bombs
Like drums, constant, maddening
I hear a scuttle and sit up
A rat is on my bed, creeping slowly
I push it off and it lands hard
On the floor, it scuttles to a mouldy cup

It's morning now
I hardly slept
I stand up and get dressed
My feet send a pain up my leg
I collapse onto my bed
I remove my shoes
And what I see, I dread

'I have trench foot.'
I tell the officer
He says, 'You'll live'
But will I?
I'm going out there again
To kill another, with family and friends
I can't stand this pain

I'm wandering through the fog
A gun in my hand
I hear shots from each direction
Right, left, up, down
And then it strikes
The bullet in my chest
It's like I'm laying on spikes

I'm on the floor now
The darkness closing in
I whisper for one last time
'I'll be in peace at last.'

Sarah Gilby (13)
Tollbar Business & Enterprise College, Grimsby

War Poetry

The guns had been booming constantly for 48 hours,
But suddenly they stopped,
Immediately we knew what was coming,
The push,
Time to go over the top,
The guns were silent,
A sound I hadn't heard in a long time,
They stopped because not even the
Politicians would risk killing their own men,
Those b******s.

They sent us here to die,
But not for our country,
But for the greed of the politicians,
The whistle went, we jumped over the top,
But I was blown right back,
My fate sealed,
I began to think,
Think of my life back home,
My life . . .
Seems so insignificant compared to all these dying,
Because of this war.

Connah Burnett (13)
Tollbar Business & Enterprise College, Grimsby

World War I – Walking Through Hell

Anger, panic, chaos running rife,
As shrapnel whistles overhead,
The last thing many will hear.
Screams of pain, cursing, gunshots, fear,
Bloodstains the ground,
The only real colour in this black and grey hell,
Rodents scurry between the corpses of many a brave man,
They say war is glorious,
What do they know, my friend?
What do they know?

The order to charge, no-man's-land awaits,
Soldiers climbing, ready to run.
The wounded stay behind, still yearning to do their part,
As death draws ever closer.
The rest stagger through the mist, rifles clutched tightly,
Waiting for the inevitable sleep,
But wanting to go out like troopers,
Ready to make the ultimate sacrifice.

Matthew Snelling (13)
Tollbar Business & Enterprise College, Grimsby

Trench

You stand there all alone
You just wanna go home
Guns blazing
In no-man's-land

Little hairy rodents
Crawling along the floor
They are squeaking
But there's no freaking

Rotting flesh
Is so not fresh
There is a lot of stench
As you lay across the bench.

Tom Pestell (13)
Tollbar Business & Enterprise College, Grimsby

Island

The plane crashes
It is on fire
It is blazing
It is raining
We are in pain
We are deserted
We might not live the night

The sea crashes against the plane
As the trees move in the breeze
In the freezing weather
On this deserted island
The clouds are moving over us
The sharks are hungry
The snakes are rattling
And we want to escape.

Tom Scott (12)
Tollbar Business & Enterprise College, Grimsby

Surviving

On the plane,
Nothing to do,
Sat with my friends,
I'm excited too,
One lousy book
And a TV,
Yet nothing's on,
Someone talk to me!

The plane has crashed,
We're the survivors,
Nothing in sight,
But the six of us,
Eating coconuts,
Trying to chase,
But all we get is monkey butts!

Faye Burke (12)
Tollbar Business & Enterprise College, Grimsby

God Has Wounded Me

God has wounded me
I must flee
I miss my wife
I feel something being drained like the blood of my life
I hate the rats
I wish we had cats

Down in no-man's-land
Men are dying as sand flows through my hand
I hear them
Those cruel, vicious men
As they are tortured by your hand
Down in no-man's-land

We eat on our backs
I would like to give them a smack
How many more will they kill
Like money falling out of a till?
Do you think you could last?
Like they kill you so fast

You wouldn't like the smell of my feet
I would love to get into the heat
What are we doing this for?
Even old men ask
Why are we doing this task?
I shall love you
And leave you
God has wounded me
I must flee.

Robert Shepherd (13)
Tollbar Business & Enterprise College, Grimsby

War Poem

The bombs were dropping overhead,
Sky's bright yellow on a winter's night,
Enemy fighting, blood flying,
Children hurting and do you hear them?

People shooting from overhead,
War soldiers not being fed,
No-man's-land was now dead man's land,
Full of corpses and pools of blood.

Politicians think it's good
For Queen and country,
Soldiers' boots full of mud,
Soldiers are dying now,
Being shot, being murdered,
They are dying for no good reason.

Why is there war?
What is it for?
These young people dying
Because they are trying.
The bombs were dropping overhead,
Sky's bright yellow on a winter's night,
Rats crawling underneath trenches,
Smells are climbing the wooden fences,
Soldiers' nightmares in the day,
The sky was red in May,
As they lay.

Sophia Pearce (13)
Tollbar Business & Enterprise College, Grimsby

Soldier's Last Words

Decaying corpses lay rotting in mud,
Rats feasted off the meat and blood.
Shrapnel shells screech through the air,
Reminds us of what's out there.

As we trudged on through day and night,
As we trudged on through mud, knee-height.
Everyone was awake and ready,
Everyone was scared and steady.

But eventually as time went by,
Our feet began to slowly die,
But we weren't allowed to stop,
Until we'd found a safe-enough spot.

'Alas!' we finally stop and rest
And hoping it was for the best,
We closed our eyes and tried to snooze,
But because of this it made us lose.

'But lose?' you ask and wonder why,
'We won the war, why tell a lie?'
But, you see that wasn't the thing,
Because instead we lost everything.

We lost our legs, our arms, our eyes,
We lost our homes, we lost our lives.

Amber Roe-Gammon (13)
Tollbar Business & Enterprise College, Grimsby

The Island Poem

Waves swallowing rocks and eating the island bit by bit
Birds wandering the island's wonders
The palm trees swaying like exotic dancers
Tropical animals their colours gleam in the sky
Delicious bittersweet fruit dropping off plants
The coral just like an aquatic rainforest
With the fishes as its swimming tourists.

Michael Fowler (12)
Tollbar Business & Enterprise College, Grimsby

Another Day

Another day, another day in Hell,
What will it bring?
Lying in the trench,
Waiting for the next bomb to go off.
Waiting for the next
Screams to be heard.
Crawling in the trench,
Crawling past my old friends
Who now lie rotting in the mud.
Rats scurrying about feasting
On the dead bodies.
The smell of urine and blood
Waft through the air.
Bullets and shrapnel screech
Above my head as the enemies fire.
Soldiers keep falling in front of me
As bombs and grenades explode nearby.
I lift my head, I fall and
Everything goes black.

Chris Wilson (14)
Tollbar Business & Enterprise College, Grimsby

War

The trenches' walls all brown and muddy,
Just like the war, it's cold and bloody.
As a young man's feet just rot and bleed,
He marches to camp, half dead, but in the lead
And here again they sit and pray
That life will be over one day.

Flares shoot up overhead,
They light up the bodies and piles of the dead,
Like cards, bodies are stacked ready to be taken away,
As the sun starts to rise to form a new day,
Love letters, diaries and cards are scattered,
Forever memories will always matter.

Roseanne-Marie Turner (13)
Tollbar Business & Enterprise College, Grimsby

War

We sit here in this pool of death
Talking about our loves
For one moment we are in peace forgetting about the sounds
For one moment we talk about life at home
For one moment in peace

The peace is broken by the voice, 'Gas, gas!'
We run to our ports to get our gas masks
One young lad who looks about 17
He trips and people trample on him
He doesn't get up

Tears flow out of my eyes
The gas clears we can breathe again
I fall and cry about the terror
We are all scared
We want to go home

Now we sit waiting for the whistle
It's happening so fast
Now we sit talking about our loves
Now we sit talking about our friends
Now we sit waiting for the whistle

The whistle was blown
We jump and run
My friends around me are dying
I fall in pain
I lay in my blood

My family is in my head
They are crying
Everything is quiet
I lay in my blood.

William Frisby (13)
Tollbar Business & Enterprise College, Grimsby

My War Poem

I'm sitting here in my trench now,
Hungry and cold,
The bombardments outside
Going over and over in my head
The foul smell of urine and the dampness
I just want to go home

The place is just infested
With frogs, lice and rats
They give us diseases and pain
I'm going insane
I'm just waiting for something to happen
Anything! I just can't bear it anymore

I'm missing my friends and family
I can't describe how much I do
And the conditions that I'm in are just unbearable
I just want to go back home

The whistle has been blown now
We're going over the top
Into no-man's-land
All of us men worried
Hoping we'll come out heroes

The sky is lit up
All of us are running and shooting
Feeling weak, I stop
I look down
Blood is dripping from me
I fall to the ground.

Loren Wykes (13)
Tollbar Business & Enterprise College, Grimsby

The Blunder

Standing still to stop and stare
Sabres flashing through all bare
Cutting through the smoky air
Charging into Satan's lair

Corpses falling to the ground
Bodies dying all around
Longing to hear a happy sound
Cannon fodder has been found

As the horse and hero fall
Some survivors still stand tall
Try to get behind the wall
Of the cannon and the ball

The biggest blunder has been made
For now six hundred have been slayed
The hardest game has now been played
Just from orders that were obeyed.

Jessica Blake (14)
Tollbar Business & Enterprise College, Grimsby

War Poem

It's my turn to go next,
Over that trench wall.
I sit anxiously
For the commander's call.

The commander shouts me
Over to him,
'Get over that wall lad.'
Duty calls.

'Go on lad!
Your family would want you to
Do it for them
And go fight and kill.'

Ross Raworth (13)
Tollbar Business & Enterprise College, Grimsby

War Poem

'Wake up, wake up!'
Another day has come,
Not one cool, copper, clean cup.
Soldiers' legs, soldiers' arms, soldiers' heads,
Still frozen in their beds,
The soldiers' hearts still live on.

'Dinner, dinner!'
Gladly the time has come,
No time to stop,
The cannons are calling,
The sandbags are falling!
The soldiers' hearts still live on.

'Rats, rats!'
The captain is calling,
The bread has gone,
The egg is burning.
People killing, people dying, people crying,
The soldiers' hearts have now gone.

Lucy Lowe (13)
Tollbar Business & Enterprise College, Grimsby

Vietnam War

The war in Vietnam was full of woe,
Young men from both sides fought toe to toe,
They fought and fought, eyes filled with fear,
So frightened, they couldn't shed a tear.
Their guns used so much, they really got hot,
They fired and fired, not knowing who they had shot,
This war went on for 25 years,
Their war was over, then there were tears.
The years in the jungle sometimes alone,
Only the lucky ones returned home.

Danielle Nilsson (13)
Tollbar Business & Enterprise College, Grimsby

War Poem

1914, another war has started,
From my family I must be parted!
Last thing I see is my sweetheart crying,
I think she's scared of me dying!

I'm in the trench now,
The siren bell sounds,
Off to no-man's-land we must go,
My brothers frantically are running round!

Battle has begun,
Without a moment to think,
There's a boy standing there,
No more, after I blink!

The battle's now ended,
We're back in the trench.
The other team surrendered,
Until the next event!

Off to sleep I go,
I feel so low,
Some of my brothers are dead,
I wonder who'll be next?

Last thing at night,
We all nodded off to sleep,
Or maybe have something to eat,
Until the bright morning light.

Battle again has begun,
Up the trench ladders we climb,
After the siren bell rung,
Peer my head out . . . *bang!*
My brother is shot dead!

Holding back tears,
Must not start crying,
I turn round and a bullet goes through me,
I'm now scared of dying.

1914, another war started,
From my family I was parted.
Last thing I remember is my sweetheart crying,
I think she was scared of me dying!

Vicky Blewitt (13)
Tollbar Business & Enterprise College, Grimsby

Another Day Goes By

Hearing all the ghost stories,
Reminds me of home,
All I see is black and red,
Instead of my nice warm bed.

How do they know?
How do they know?
What pain I am going through,
Every day to just stay alive.

Rats, bodies, blood and mud,
Sea, grass, trees and sky,
I just don't know anymore,
Which one I like.

Trenches get filled with gas,
We struggle for our lives,
Men falling to the ground,
Oh, it's just another corpse.

Nearly the end of the war now,
It's soon time to go home,
Please Lord, please Lord,
Let me go home alive.

Kerry Bull (13)
Tollbar Business & Enterprise College, Grimsby

Great War

It all starts with politics,
Franz Ferdinand was shot.
Suddenly the butchers were sent to the trenches,
Sometimes long enough to rot.

Rats ruled the trench, with the threat of Weil's disease,
Bombarded by artillery,
Two days at a time.

The ghost story is turning me insane,
Even though it would normally sound lame.
The guns scare me just the same,
However, they aren't so lame.

I wish I was at home,
Rushing to turn on the wireless,
Not to put on my gas mask,
Now my trench food is as big as my fear,
As big as my fear of rats and Weil's disease,
Finally, the whistle is here.

They came,
Running for our trench,
Running for an unknown cause,
Running for their lives, in the rain.

Bullets and barbed wire our only protection,
In this chaotic scene of desperation,
Men fall down wounded,
On their way to Heaven,
Now it's my turn to get away from Hell,
I welcomed the bullet.

Alex Blanchard (13)
Tollbar Business & Enterprise College, Grimsby

The Island

Am I dead or alive?
Alive
And what is this soft butter pressing
Against my cheek?
Nope, nope just messy, rough sand,
Where am I? Home?
No, on an island.

Sun burning my skin off,
Sharp, tall grass itching
And scratching my arms and legs.
Unusual noises and sounds,
Rough, woody ground making
Crunching and crackling noises,
For every step I make.

At last green cool grass,
Nope, a green muddy swamp,
Rain! Just what I needed!
Five minutes later I got more,
For what I asked, a monsoon.
Need high ground and again
I get more for what I asked for, a volcano.

At last a lifeguard to rescue me,
Lots of questions that are unanswered,
Where was I? What was it?
Was it just a fantasy or reality?

Rachel Smith (12)
Tollbar Business & Enterprise College, Grimsby

A New Dawn, A New Day!

I write from the battlefield of the great push,
With thousands of unburied around me,
Soon it was going to be my turn,
But why should you people at home not know?

Death was a constant companion to those serving in the line,
Even when no raid or attack was launched
Or defended against,
I thank those who created but one helmet,
Gas protector and bayonet,
Why should you people at home not show?

'Go, go and don't turn back,
It's your destiny, don't slack!'
We looked at each other,
I was faced with the option of going on our separate ways
Or else engaging in hand to hand fighting
But why should you people at home not know?

I wondered who would be the first to decide
Me or him?
I was scared, but he had no fear in his eyes whatsoever,
It was his turn,
I fell into a swimming pool of my own blood,
Never knowing, never showing,
Why should the people at home not know?

Emma Haagensen (13)
Tollbar Business & Enterprise College, Grimsby

On The Island

It was a night just right,
To give you a fright.
Lightning struck,
We weren't in luck.
It hit the plane,
What a shame.
The plane went down,
I thought it might drown.
I swam to the island,
The island, the island.
The volcano, the trees,
They were the bee's knees.
The hard, strong, mighty,
Volcano towers up above,
I was looking at it, when someone gave me a shove.
We went to the hot spring,
There we felt like kings.
I said, 'Who will look for food?'
James said, 'I will look for food, Dude.'
So out he went into the jungle,
On the island, the island, the island,
A helicopter came chopping away,
We were safe, they had found us.

Sam Burdett (12)
Tollbar Business & Enterprise College, Grimsby

War Poem

Bombs dropping . . . *bang, bang, bang,*
Hearts beating . . . *bdum, bdum, bdum,*
Heads hurting . . . *ow, ow, ow,*
Eyes blinking . . . *blink, blink, blink,*
The whole world goes quiet and it's over.

People kill and people die,
Children hurt and leave them to cry,
Then you practise what you preach,
But then you turn the other cheek,
Father help us,
Send some guidance from above,
People got me questioning,
When's this war going to be over?

Bodies, blood, weapons and lice,
All over, laying on the ground,
People crying and people dying,
Families and friends all around,
Waiting to see who will be crowned.

Abbie Blythin & Aimee Burgess (13)
Tollbar Business & Enterprise College, Grimsby

My Island

On the island there are lots of sharks,
But there is no room for playing parks!

The big dark hole is very deep,
So only have a little peep!

Cross the rickety bridge if you dare,
Watch out though, you might get a big scare!

The slimy swamp is very long,
So watch out for the mighty pong!

Katie Huddleston (12)
Tollbar Business & Enterprise College, Grimsby

The Island

This island is
Hot and bright
The sea is
Glistening as the
Boats pass by
You can hear the
Waterfall and the
Volcano spluttering
You can smell the
Sweet salty air
The sand falls through
Your fingers
There are a few animals
And a sea monster but
The rest is deserted.

Emma Dewires (13)
Tollbar Business & Enterprise College, Grimsby

World War I

Guns spitting, bombs flying,
Beasts that feast on the deceased,
A few things that plagued the trenches.

Blood bathed bodies that litter the ditch,
Thrown away as if rubbish,
Lost their lives for their countries
But gained nothing back.

Gas covered the land like a green fog,
Taking the lives of those who cross its path,
Fumbling and clumsily putting on gas masks.

No one will ever know what the war was like,
Except the people that lived through it,
But make sure that you remember the ones that didn't.

Sam Smith (13)
Tollbar Business & Enterprise College, Grimsby

Crash Landing

On the plane,
Very excited,
Going to Australia,
To watch Man United.

But wait a second,
The plane's going funny,
Bouncing around,
Like an insane bunny.

Going down,
At the speed of sound,
30,000 feet
Above the ground.

The attendants said
'We are all going to die,
So put your head between your legs
And kiss your butt goodbye!'

Sam Strandt (12)
Tollbar Business & Enterprise College, Grimsby

War

'RPG' shouted Sarge,
Dirt, rubble and corpses cascaded,
Like a waterfall,
From the smoke-filled sky.
Fighting next to new families,
As they get picked off by the opposition.

Round their feet the water flows,
Waiting for the order to go 'over the top',
Knowing that some might not survive the push,
When the night falls,
The flares go up,
It doesn't matter how they feel,
The slaughter never stops.

Joshua Saxton (13)
Tollbar Business & Enterprise College, Grimsby

The War

His troops set off with their guns in the air,
As the sound of shells drop everywhere,
There they crept on the battlefield,
Hiding in trenches or further afield.

His troops stand silent,
As they could not cry,
Watching their fellow friends,
Lying there to die.

There in the trench with the
Rats he did lie,
The smell of death was
Extremely close by.

His troops marched the bloody field,
Where men lay injured or dead,
As he marched on, inside he was dying,
The pain, the trauma, the numbness inside.

He carried on as he started crying,
He thought of home and wished he was there.

Jessica Humphreys (13)
Tollbar Business & Enterprise College, Grimsby

The Island!

T is for being *so* terrified
H is for horrible, lonely nights
E is for ensuring I will get off this island

I is for the ice cube that I feel like every day
S is for scary sounds in the bush
L is for living and holding onto my brush,
A is for anxious sitting by the fire,
N is for no food, having to hunt,
D is for death that I fear every second for me and my family.

Sarah Shambrook (12)
Tollbar Business & Enterprise College, Grimsby

The Aeroplane

I've never been on an aeroplane,
The waiting's been driving me insane!
I've never waited for a flight,
I've never travelled late at night.

I've never flown,
I've never flown
And I am frightened to the bone,
How does it float? How does it fly?

If we went on a boat,
Maybe then we'll stay afloat.

We give our bags, we read our mags,
I hate flying, I was nearly crying,
My sister was, all because
We were scared, until we heard
The captain say, 'We're here!'

That was then and this is now,
I don't know how,
I don't know why,
But right now I love to fly.

Roseanne Heinzman (13)
Tollbar Business & Enterprise College, Grimsby

My Poem

Oh no, we've had a crash
I feel rather boiling hot
We must have come in with a big bash
But we can't feel a lot

At least we have a lot of water
But it's infested with sharks and all sorts
So we can't get much of that water
That water that is all around us.

Daniel Adamson (12)
Tollbar Business & Enterprise College, Grimsby

It's A Day!

It's a hot day,
Walking around,
Trees are swaying,
Seas are waving.

Clouds start to close
In on us,
We are lost,
Winds pick up.

I start to dread
What might happen while
We settle down to bed,
It's thunder and lightning.

It's a cold day,
Under shelter,
Trees are falling,
Seas are roaring.

Rebecca Clayton (12)
Tollbar Business & Enterprise College, Grimsby

Terror Island

The wind was blowing
The sea was flowing
The lamps were glowing
The boats were rowing
The waves were crashing
The cliffs were smashing
The cabins were creaking
The families were meeting

A riot of people ran around
The lamps of the town flickered out
The town was doomed without a doubt.

Ian Fowler (12)
Tollbar Business & Enterprise College, Grimsby

War Poem

Sitting in this wet, muddy trench,
I think about painting my garden fence,
I promised Mary I would do it,
That was when I was well and fit.

Rifles shooting far and near,
As a rotting pong takes up the air,
I think it's that deceased man's hair.

My clothes are wet and feet all damp,
Without the mention of being cramped,
I hate this horrid, stupid camp.

I wish I could go home today,
Or tell me I'll see friends again,
I know I could die any time soon,
As I face the unpredictable doom.

Beth Mitchell (13)
Tollbar Business & Enterprise College, Grimsby

War

War, what does it mean?
People killing just like machines
The enemy, one gun and you
Load the gun, cock it back, point and kill

The blood slowly running down your face
As your partner dies in battle
Bloodstains on your face while trying not to cry
You feel angered and want revenge
But can't do anything

They said the war was nearly over
That was a month ago
We get told to just keep firing
Deep down you feel outraged
Another life wasted.

Daniel Sampson (13)
Tollbar Business & Enterprise College, Grimsby

The Ruthless Germans

It's the story of us, we British roar,
To stop the Germans, preventing the war,
Rats were problems, so were mice,
Carrying diseases, making a crisis,
Death words march into the German's minds,
Making trenches, barbed wire behind,
Smells were also problems too,
Smell too much and it could kill you

Fire and fire, over gain
Bloodshed and Hell, that was the same,
Germans running over the hills,
Aiming their guns, licence to kill,
Travelling no-man's-land, without permission,
Trying to stop us completing our mission,
Inside the trenches nowhere to hide,
Germans coming, 'Going outside!'

We think about home every day,
Ferdinand shot, 'Serbia pay!'
Thinking of what to do next, then and then,
Germans coming into our den,
Germans hearing one of our calls,
They ran and ran, like a pack of wolves.
'What should I do next? Where should I go?
Going to Hell or to home?'

I felt worried, I laughed, scared,
I felt sad, from good to bad.
Death and death, that was the same,
Super explosions, Germans to blame,
By the time it has finished, all was gone,
This was real, not any old con,
It was the end, or so we thought,
This was our story, Germany born.

Adam Clowery (13)
Tollbar Business & Enterprise College, Grimsby

My Aggression

As we stormed into their village
Their watcher ran off to warn the people
I just noticed him out of the corner of my eye
So I turned round and shot at him
I didn't use a silencer like none of us
But that was the mistake we made -
We didn't know there were caves below us.

We stormed into the village
I saw all the shocked faces of the gooks
We all searched around finding people hidden in caves
And we found lots of weapons with these gooks
I found a big family in a cave, hiding lots of weapons
'Get out, get out, or I'll bomb you.'

A few of the family got out
But I lost my patience, I just couldn't wait any longer
'Fire in the hole.' I dropped my grenade in the hole
Bang! The gooks were screaming their heads off
I couldn't stand the noise -
It just sounded like crying babies
The noise annoyed me too much
I swung round with my gun with aggression
That knocked down one of the gooks' family.

Nathan Tyas (13)
Tollbar Business & Enterprise College, Grimsby

War

Sitting in the still silence staring into the darkness,
In the jungle I never sleep well,
The creatures of the night are always alive to keep me awake,
How I thought the crickets annoyed me at home,
And how I wish I was there right now,
Things on my mind like what tomorrow will bring,
And whether I dread to think about it.
Raiding innocent villages,
Innocent . . .
Or what we thought were innocent.
As the sun rises, men start to awaken,
Have a cigarette and are ready to go.
We plough through the trees and wilderness,
Minding our every move because they,
They . . .
Could be there watching each of our steps.
Twice they have sneaked men away,
Our men . . .
And twice they have succeeded in tricking us.
They are so silent, no one even notices,
Our men have gone,
Until we find them tied to trees . . .

Lauren Beer (13)
Tollbar Business & Enterprise College, Grimsby

Poor Mrs Brown

Poor Mrs Brown got a telegram yesterday,
She showed it to me last night.
How I dreaded that knock on the door,
For news of an injury or worse.
Would I know the person who returned?
Would he survive the trauma of war
To live a normal life again?

He came home a month ago,
But there is a stranger in the house,
Haunted by the shellfire and gas.
Calling out for friends who are no longer there.
Restless nights are a regular thing
And nightmares come too often.
He talks of the trenches every now and then,
About the smell that made him sick
And the cat-sized rats that would chew at his feet.

I remember the day he left,
That last passionate embrace,
Where is the man I used to know?
How I envy Mrs Brown!

Charlotte Cooper (13)
Tollbar Business & Enterprise College, Grimsby

War Poetry

We built the fences
And all the trenches
To hide and protect
But with the smell
And the little food
Really the trenches are no good

On my back I lay
Please stop this war I pray
But still people are dying
And I am still crying
As the guns are still firing

I've seen the worst
The world is cursed
How did this ever happen?

On my back I lay
Please stop this war I pray
But still people are dying
And I am still crying
As the guns are still firing.

Miriam Samy (13)
Tollbar Business & Enterprise College, Grimsby

Six Feet From Hell

They said it would be 'glorious',
They said they would be 'proud',
They shoved me off a truck
And into the gates of Hell.

The warm grip of the rifle,
The cold stench of the blood.
The cry of death,
The one way march.

'Over the top!'
The Devil's words,
Machine gun fire,
The Devil's laugh.

The sight,
The stench.
It was enough to
Make a man go mad.

Mike Law (13)
Tollbar Business & Enterprise College, Grimsby

The Bridge

Shell after shell, the German artillery pounded our lines
The deafening silence almost got me to sleep until
Boom! A shell blew a chunk out of the crumbling sandbags
And a big chunk almost hit me as it flew past and sunk into the slop
Suddenly our ears stopped focusing on the shellfire
And turned to the squeaks and roars of an oncoming battalion
Of German tanks crossing the bridge

'Quick boys! Piats at the ready.'
We jumped for our rocket launchers
'Ready, aim, fire!'
The atmosphere filled with smoke from the barrels of our guns
As the smoke cleared we saw not only the tanks in the river
But also half the bridge.

Jordan Baxter (13)
Tollbar Business & Enterprise College, Grimsby

The Great War

The mud has now dried
The tears have now cried
The sun begins to rise
Over the blood-red poppies

But I am still in the horror
The horror of war
My eyes see nothing
But of the men that once were

Yet I feel at home here
In the muddy sludge
I see body parts around my ankles
In what was no-man's-land

In the trenches I longed to be home
With my mother, my father, my brother

My brothers, born lame and could not fight
Sometimes I wish I was like that

Every November I used to waddle to the old statue
The statue that is titled: 'The Great War'

To me the war wasn't great at all

What is great about the silence
The deafening silence
The cry and wails of my friends
As they slowly die?

Some days I could stand the screaming
Some days I had to be held back
So I didn't bounce off the tiny walls of the trench

I ask you my friend, what do you think is great about that?

Amy Hodgson (13)
Tollbar Business & Enterprise College, Grimsby

War Time

The war continued!
Even more bloodshed and death was on the cards.
I killed a German fighter, but I'm not proud.
The day was a dim and heartfelt genre.
Not even a smile was made!
I can't complain though.

Politicians!
They are the people who have made us into these fragile characters,
Forcing us into this glorified war of blood and sweat.
What they do at home is at a far better standard
Of that we are doing now.
They said we were going on holiday!

No-man's-land is a scare!
Bodies lying dead,
Paralysed with no hope at all.
I'm petrified!
I hope for me and my families' sake
I somehow survive this dreadful decade
In England's history!

Matthew Nicholson (13)
Tollbar Business & Enterprise College, Grimsby

War Poem

Every morning they wake up to the same old place.
They didn't get much sleep last night because of a night raid.
Dead bodies surround them; every day this they have to face.
In a wagon they put them, on top of each other they're laid.

Some not quite dead yet but soon they will be.
Some men watch it go, it could be them next time.
Is this their destiny?
If some could live through this, it would not be a crime,
They could come out of this but far from fine.

Rations - just enough to keep some alive.
It's the same food nearly every day.
On their heated bodies lice thrive.
Men spending hours to keep these disease-ridden
Creatures away.

War they are at, some want the glory.
Some have been made to go.
Some just children, falling for a fairytale story.
What these men have had to face
Most of us won't even know.

Lauren Grice (14)
Tollbar Business & Enterprise College, Grimsby

My Poem

Gunshots echoed through me like thunder
So loud it dazed me
If you could hear the repetitive flares
You would no longer be able to stand fireworks
Or the whistle from a kettle

Corpses lay on the ground
Every face had the same expression
Terror and pain
But that was nothing compared to the expression
On the poor men barely living

Not only do I have to live with the external scars
I've still got the scars in my head
Which will never fade away
If I survive the war
There's no chance I can go back to the way I was!

Laura King (13)
Tollbar Business & Enterprise College, Grimsby

War!

The trench is cold and muddy,
With rats and isn't very sunny.

Outside is loud and misty,
I'd rather have a bottle of whisky.

Smells of mouldy, dead rats,
People will just hit them with their bats.

I wish I was at home,
Lying in my bed all alone.

But, I'm here in the trench,
Near a cold and muddy bench.

Waiting very, very, very long . . .
Thinking what is going on?

Sarah Milner
Tollbar Business & Enterprise College, Grimsby

The War!

Why is the war happening?
It is horrific.
It may be for my country,
I know I hate the politicians,
Why should I do it for them?
I'll do it for my family back home in Grimsby.

People are dying every day,
Germans and Englishmen are dying,
Dead bodies all around us,
People always firing,
With blood always dripping,
No one is safe, not even you politicians.

I stood there with my general,
Think of good times,
But all we could think of was getting out alive,
I wish I could be back home,
Spending time with my family,
That's all I should think about not death, no nothing,
So come on you English, let's do it for folks back home!

In the trenches men are scared,
No one is safe, not even from the rats.
The smell is horrific,
It's so unbearable.
Just like looking at a trench foot,
All I can do is keep on fighting,
I must remain positive,
For you, family back home.

Lewis Wressell (13)
Tollbar Business & Enterprise College, Grimsby

The Horrors Of War

As I reluctantly lie in the rat-infested trench,
I repeatedly think of my old wooden bench.
My knees are sore, I have wet feet,
Just like every other soldier I meet.

At home the bench is a favourite place of mine,
As I used to watch the sunset while drinking wine.
I pray my time will not drain away,
As long as I sit on my bench next May.

Rifle shots are a regular sound,
All around this muddy mound.
The stench of fear and death is strong,
This is not a place where I belong.

I hope this war will end very soon
And I can go home with my platoon.
Some of the enemy are only young boys,
Having to bear this dreadful noise.

Felicity Tuxworth (14)
Tollbar Business & Enterprise College, Grimsby

The Poppy

The world is a bitter place full of arguments and wars,
But the government's in charge now and this place is full of laws.
We've had war after war and still haven't learnt our lesson;
I've learnt much about the war but still have one more question.

Why did these wars begin?
Is it because we are stupid humans who always get what we want
Or is it because we can't be bothered to talk and sort things out?
I feel guilty for all those men who died out on the battlefields
For just one person to get what they wanted.
Many people were hurt and died in that period of time,
But for each life that was taken one poppy grew.
The poppy is now the flower of remembrance
And has been known for that since the days of the war,
With its delicate petals the poppy is as beautiful as life itself.

Alix Roberts (13)
Tollbar Business & Enterprise College, Grimsby

Sunset Island

Wild in the country with snakes
In the grass,
Lizards and crocodiles are a mass,
Monkeys and lemurs take it at ease,
But after all they are the bee's knees,
Parrots squawking to their heart's delight,
Possums get a sudden fright.

The sun is setting in the west,
Soon the island will be at rest,
The palm trees gently sway to and fro,
Where coconuts drop down below.

Particles of sand are swept out to sea,
The barracuda swims so gently,
Sharks circle close to shore,
Oh my gosh, I think they want more!

James Brockbank (12)
Tollbar Business & Enterprise College, Grimsby

War

War
In the trenches, feet drowning in water,
Shells dropping everywhere, drumming from the mortar,
The squelching boots silently sticking to bloody sores.

War
Out on the treacherous battlefield full of rotting bodies,
Rats the size of cats, spreading round different disease,
Men mentally dying - they cannot take much more.

War
Frightened men swelling with tonnes of emotion,
The bright wide eyes spying on elevation.
Why do people start these wars?
They treat it like a chore.
Why don't people realise
That the only key to war is peace?

Jonathan Bishop (13)
Tollbar Business & Enterprise College, Grimsby

The Ace Car

The ace car is parked,
Outside my house.
Everyone was staring,
Even the mouse!

The ace rims
Were really high.
When the car started up,
There was no time to say bye!

He always won the races,
It made him rich!
Blue flames from the exhaust,
As he flicked the NOS switch.

You could hear it
From a mile away.
Sounds like a volcano
People may say.

The neon glow,
In the shiny gold.
Before the car was done up,
It could never be sold.

He has no house,
Just an apartment
And he just put a computer,
In the glove compartment.

When the cops come round,
He's ready to bail.
Still checking out the TV,
In the middle of the steering wheel.

The music is booming,
As the speakers are big.
When he goes past the fancy dress,
They all lose their wigs.

The ace car
Is black and gold,
The record for fastest car
He still holds.

Everyone loves going in
His pimped-up ride.
The others who are embarrassed
Try to hide.

The car is the most popular
In the town,
If cars were kings,
It would win the crown.

His car has a birthday
And it blows its own candles.
More gizmo in the boot,
That most cars can handle.

James Regan (12)
Tollbar Business & Enterprise College, Grimsby

Poem About Sport

Running is great,
Because you lose weight,
It stops you being late
And you don't look a state.

Boxing is fun,
But you can hurt your tum,
No boxers cry
But some do die.

Swimming is cool,
You go in a pool,
You jump off a diving board
And go under the water.

Gymnastics are fantastic,
You can do forward rolls,
You can become really flexible
And you can swing on metal poles.

Louise Cowan (12)
Tollbar Business & Enterprise College, Grimsby

My Special Island

The beautiful curly hair of the mermaids
Shines in the sun.
The strong tall trees,
Sway in the breeze.
My small footprints,
Sink into the sand, step by step.
The mountains stand tall,
As the mountain lions run for their prey.
Today the treasure has been found,
As I'm chased by a strange sound.
The caves are dark,
That I have to sleep in every night, all alone.
Volcanoes pour out lava right to haunted house,
Even demons are killed.
The woodland is an excellent place to play,
Even on a very dreary day.
The spooky graveyard at night,
Makes it such a scary sight.
Tonight I'll spend time with mermaids,
Until I fall asleep,
For the last time we ever meet.

Alicia Jenkins (12)
Tollbar Business & Enterprise College, Grimsby

The Perfect Puss!

As the perfect puss walks down the catwalk
Her coat gleams
She walks and everyone shines
With the colour of her fur
As she spins, her pearly eyes beam
As silence creeps over the crowd
You can hear her purr
The crowd is not making a sound
While there is love all around!

Abi Read (12)
Tollbar Business & Enterprise College, Grimsby

Spy Poem

L9 is the coolest guy,
He is the master of disguise
And people think he's very wise.
He's good with a gun
And he thinks it's fun
To chase people on the run.

His worst enemy is the Scream,
He is cruel and very mean.
He's everywhere but seldom seen,
L9 went on a mission to Iraq,
To find Scream and bring him back,
Or MI5 would give him the sack.

Eventually he tracked him down
And brought him back to his home town
And Scream called him a stupid clown.
That is the story of cool L9,
The greatest spy of all time.

Lewis Barker (11)
Tollbar Business & Enterprise College, Grimsby

Sea Poem

Stepping stones may break my bones
As I lay on the sand a key pushes at my leg
In the distance I lay eyes on a treasure chest
So I get up to go and get it
I finally get there but find it's only a mirage
I look out to sea, I see a whirlpool
I see a boat and stuff in it, it is scary
So I run away in terror,
I see a plane window, so I use it as a mirror,
I see palm trees waving in the breeze,
Unfortunately the breeze made me freeze.

Josh Shipp (12)
Tollbar Business & Enterprise College, Grimsby

My Puppy

My cute little puppy,
Playing with his ball,
He runs around,
Until he sprawls onto the ground.

The puppy-dog eyes he gives me,
Makes me want to smile with glee.

My little puppy chases his tail,
But will never ever catch it,
He tries and tries until he decides,
That butterflies are a better prize.

My gorgeous little 'fluff ball',
He's new to the world,
Shaking and whimpering,
In the corner he's curled,
He's after reassurance,
Cos there's nothing more frightening,
Than a stormy night
Filled with thunder and lightning.

Chloe Wraith (12)
Tollbar Business & Enterprise College, Grimsby

Swiftly

As I walk along the beautiful sand
With the sand in-between my toes
I admire the beautiful island
Suddenly a tingle goes up my nose

As I go on an adventurous hunt
I climb up a tree
To see what I can see
As I look into the distance
I can see the sea.

Rachel Parkin (12)
Tollbar Business & Enterprise College, Grimsby

Shop Till You Drop

Bleep, bleep, the sound of the till
Adding onto my credit card bill

Spending all my hard earned cash
Another shop I've got to dash

Squandering money I have not got
Never mind, I will buy the lot

Skirt, top and trousers too
Who cares as long as it's new?

Fabulous buying in the shop
Now I'm tired and ready to drop.

Leigha Knight (12)
Tollbar Business & Enterprise College, Grimsby

Golden Dust

Golden paths of silence lay ahead
Crossing waves of peaceful colour
Mystery was ahead!
Scary doom headed for me
The perfection was smashed!
Silent gardens flew ahead, curving and twisting
Was I in a fairy tale of woods and silence?
Traces of magic, with a hint of silence tipped
The spooks of ancient tribes!
The tomb of doom was like a wood
Where was the master?

Gemma Dabb (12)
Tollbar Business & Enterprise College, Grimsby

In The Middle Of No-Man's-Land

As I lie here in this pool of red liquid
With flashbacks of my family,
I hear my brothers and my mum and dad
Crying as I'm dying,
Lying here in this battlefield,
The middle of no-man's-land,
I smell the last poor dead man's rotting legs and hands.
I see the shrapnel whistling past,
Through the cloudy, smoke-filled sky.
I try to see the stars above,
But all I see is the bombs which fly.
I feel the cold, shrill air harshly
Whip past as I lie here waiting to die.
I reach out my hand to feel how bad
The wound is, but I feel nothing,
My body is numb apart from the shooting pain,
Which runs up and down my body every now and again.
The day is drawing to an end,
Soon this life will be over,
I slowly shut my weary eyes,
I take my final breath and die.
My body, my soul lies here in this battlefield,
The middle of no-man's-land.
I lie here all alone in the black ash
And flesh-filled sand.

Molly Blow (13)
Tollbar Business & Enterprise College, Grimsby

My War Poem

Rats, rats, running around
Rats, rats, surrounding the ground
The siren bell sounds
I grab my artillery

Bang, bang, overhead
Bang, bang, people dead
Seeing people ahead
Striving to no-man's-land

Retreat, retreat, it's time to retreat
Retreat, retreat, my sore feet
We all meet
Back at the trench

Splish, splash, covered in muck
Splish, splash, time to duck
Bullets everywhere I look
In the dirty trenches

Rats, rats, running around
Rats, rats, surrounding the ground
They make a sound
As I fall asleep.

Emily Fletcher (13)
Tollbar Business & Enterprise College, Grimsby